The Amazing Adventures of
MR. GRANT MONEY

Dear Reader,

Thank you for embarking on this exciting journey with "The Amazing Adventures of Mr. Grant Money." I'm thrilled to share with you the valuable insights and lessons contained within these pages, lessons that have empowered countless individuals and organizations to achieve remarkable success in their grant acquisition endeavors.

Grant funding is a powerful tool, and this book is designed to be your companion as you navigate the intricate world of grant writing. Within these stories lie not just narratives but essential lessons that will guide you toward securing funding for your projects. As you read and engage with the exercises, I hope you find inspiration and actionable strategies to elevate your grant acquisition efforts to new heights.

Throughout my career, I've had the privilege of assisting many individuals starting from ground zero, witnessing their transformation into successful grant seekers. The stories and lessons in this book encapsulate some of the crucial insights that have contributed to their achievements.

However, I must take a moment to introduce you to another invaluable resource—the "Grant Writing That Gets Funded" training. This training has been a cornerstone in the success stories of numerous students and organizations. Tailored for beginners and intermediate grant professionals, it offers clear and comprehensive guidance. Participants not only absorb my exclusive Grant Writing Success Formula but also leave with a personalized 30-Day Grant Empowerment Strategy and Grant Readiness Resource.

Our training has played a pivotal role in agencies securing substantial funding, ranging from $25,000 to millions, in a remarkably short period. You can witness some of these success stories at WowTheyDidIt.com. I am confident that with our support, you could be the next success story, unlocking a bountiful windfall of grant funding for your endeavors.

Imagine the impact on your team as they gain insights, adopt best practices, and leverage industry secrets, giving your agency a competitive edge. This training could be the pivotal factor that distinguishes you from others, ensuring you secure the grants you pursue.

As Kjeld Linstead, a past participant, expressed, "Thanks again for the grants class a few months ago... Since taking your class, I have landed nearly $4 Million in state and federal grants for the City of Redlands."

For more information about the Grant Writing That Gets Funded training, please visit GrantWritingClasses.org. You can also secure your spot by calling 1-888-293-0284. This investment in your organization's financial stability is a strategic move towards a more prosperous future.

Best Regards,

Rodney
Grant Central USA

P.S. Be sure to try our free grant training at StrategicGrantWriting.com

The Amazing Adventures of
MR. GRANT MONEY

Grant Odyssey: Mr. Grant Money's Time-Traveling Feats

VOLUME FOUR

RODNEY WALKER

Copyright © 2024, Strive Press LLC

All rights reserved. No part of the material protected by this copyright notice may be reproduced or utilized in any form or by any means, electronic or mechanical, including photocopying, recording, or by any information storage and retrieval system, without permission from the copyright owner.

Under no circumstances will any blame or legal responsibility be held against the publisher or author for any damages, reparation, or monetary loss due to the information contained within this book. Either directly or indirectly. You are responsible for your own choices, actions, and results.

For related titles and support materials, visit our online catalog at www.mrgrantmoney.com and www.grantcentralusa.com

Legal Notice:

This book is copyright-protected. This book is only for personal use. You cannot amend, distribute, sell, use, quote, or paraphrase any part of this book's content without the author's or publisher's consent.

Disclaimer Notice:

Please note the information contained within this document is for educational and entertainment purposes only. All effort has been executed to present accurate, up-to-date, reliable, and complete information. No warranties of any kind are declared or implied. Readers acknowledge that the author is not rendering legal, financial, medical, or professional advice. The content within this book has been derived from various sources. Please consult a licensed professional before attempting any techniques outlined in this book.

By reading this document, the reader agrees that under no circumstances is the author responsible for any losses, direct or indirect, which are incurred as a result of the use of the information contained within this document, including, but not limited to, — errors, omissions, or inaccuracies.

Chief Editor: Laine Minerales
Editorial Assistant: Daniel Tuano
Production Supervisor: Joerje Galo
Electronic Composition: Jairus Agoncillo
Photographer: Studio 5404
Executive Marketing Manager: Jimmy Moore

Discover the breadth of our series, encompassing a myriad of crucial topics. Delve into the realms of grant acquisition, college scholarships, entrepreneurship, social impact, philanthropy, and beyond. Unearth a treasure trove of knowledge and empowerment within our diverse collection. Explore the wealth of insights awaiting you across these transformative series.

To inquire about utilizing The Amazing Adventures of Mr. Grant Money books in the classroom, securing licensing, and exploring special pricing for bulk orders, kindly contact us at info@grantcentralusa.com.

ISBN: 978-0-9659275-4-3

Printed in the United States

Dedication

To my cherished nieces, Christina and Crystal Walker,
This book is dedicated to you both with immense love and hope for the future. As you continue to blossom into beautiful young ladies, I am filled with pride and excitement for the remarkable journey ahead. May you always carry the fine Walker legacy with grace and strength.

In you, I see the radiant light of our beloved mother, a beacon of wisdom, kindness, and resilience. I have no doubt that you will carry her legacy forward, shining brightly with the love and wisdom she passed down to us all.

With love,
Uncle Rod

PREFACE

The Adventures of Mr. Grant Money: A Journey of Transformation

In the world of grant acquisition, where dreams take flight on the wings of well-crafted proposals, where passion meets purpose, and where communities are transformed through the power of giving, I invite you to embark on a remarkable journey. These adventures are not just a recounting of tales but a testament to the evolution of a grant professional who started with the humblest of beginnings and emerged as a Master Grant Acquisition Specialist.

Over two decades in the making, these stories are a blend of my real-life experiences as a grant professional. They unfold the lessons learned, the challenges faced, and the victories achieved. From the time when I was a novice, wide-eyed and eager to write my first grant proposal, seeking a mere $25,000 for a youth development program, to the present, where I've had the privilege of assisting thousands of individuals and organizations worldwide each year, this journey is one of profound transformation.

It all began with the idea of sharing inspiring tales through a series of blog posts, offering snippets of wisdom and knowledge to those in the world of grants. Yet, as I put pen to paper, these stories took on a life of their own, weaving together to form something magical, something special. What started as a caterpillar of inspiration morphed into a butterfly waiting for you to leap onto its wings and embark on a series of captivating journeys.

This collection is intended to educate and entertain, to offer fresh ideas and insights for seasoned veterans of the grant profession, to guide and inspire newcomers, and perhaps even awaken the curiosity of a young student unaware of the incredible world of grant acquisition.

In this adventure, we'll dive into the core of grant writing, explore the depths of fundraising, and unearth the hidden treasures of effective philanthropy. We'll laugh, we'll learn, and we'll leap beyond the boundaries of the ordinary.

But at the heart of it all, this is a testament to the power of belief. For, as you'll discover, belief is the force that propels dreams into reality. As you journey through these tales, remember one word: BELIEVE!

Now, dear reader, join me as we venture forth into the world of Mr. Grant Money's adventures. Let's explore, learn, and transform together. The journey begins with a single page, and the possibilities are endless.

TABLE OF CONTENT

Introduction	8
Regal Secrets: A Royal Exchange of Philanthropic Wisdom	9
Grant Acquisition Through the Sands of Time	16
Granting Diplomatic Maneuvers: Mr. Grant Money's African Odyssey	22
The Art of Grant Money: Picasso's Philanthropic Encounter	28
Beneath the Surface: Grant Acquisition Lessons from the Silent Language of the Deep Sea	35
Scoop Diggity, Jamie Kibble, and the Scepter of Grant Wisdom	41
Gifts, Grants, and Glacial Discoveries: Mr. Grant Money at the North Pole	48
From Relativity to Funding: Mr. Grant Money's Journey	54
Mr. Grant Money's Hollywood Heist: The Golden Ticket Caper	61
Mr. Grant Money's Aussie Adventure: Outback Triumph	67
Afterward	73
About the Author	74
Boost Your Grant Game: Additional Resources	76

INTRODUCTION

Welcome back to the remarkable world of Mr. Grant Money's extraordinary adventures. As you embark on Volume 4, "Grant Odyssey," you are about to witness time-traveling feats and timeless wisdom that will take your understanding of grant acquisition to new heights.

With the titles such as "Regal Secrets," "Touchdowns and Triumphs," and "Mr. Grant Money's Aussie Adventure," you're in for a rollercoaster of experiences that stretch across continents, eras, and imagination. Each story unveils a unique facet of Mr. Grant Money's multifaceted journey, offering you insights into the diverse strategies and mindsets that fuel his unparalleled success.

The adventures that unfold in the pages ahead are not just tales but valuable lessons wrapped in engaging narratives. After each short story, you'll find exercises designed to help you implement similar strategies employed by MGM. Discussion questions will encourage you to dig deeper, while powerful quotes and a single BIG Idea from each story will resonate in your grant acquisition practices.

"Grant Odyssey" continues to be a valuable resource for a broad audience. Whether you're a grant writing instructor, a student venturing into the world of grants, a new grant writer, an experienced grant professional, a fundraiser, a grant consultant, or a representative of a nonprofit organization, you'll find inspiration and wisdom within these pages. The lessons are adaptable, relevant, and timeless, making them suitable for various sectors, including government agencies and faith-based organizations.

It's essential to clarify what this book is and what it is not. "Grant Odyssey" is not a step-by-step guide on how to write a grant. Instead, it offers something more profound. It provides an immersive adventure through the lens of Mr. Grant Money, allowing you to experience the creativity, resilience, and resourcefulness that are hallmarks of his success. You'll learn to navigate the intricate web of grant acquisition with skill, determination, and style.

As you dive into the stories that await you, remember that the lessons transcend time and space, offering you a treasure trove of grant acquisition insights. The pages of "Grant Odyssey" invite you to explore the unknown, discover the timeless, and claim your role as a grant acquisition expert.

In the words of the wise, "The journey of a thousand miles begins with a single step." As you turn the page and delve into Volume 4, you're not just taking a step; you're embarking on a remarkable odyssey. Your grant acquisition journey has reached a new dimension, where the past, present, and future merge to unlock new possibilities.

Enjoy your adventure, and remember the power word - "Elevate". As you journey through these stories, aim to elevate your grant acquisition game to new heights, just like Mr. Grant Money.

Regal Secrets: A Royal Exchange of Philanthropic Wisdom

When Prince Charles Meets Mr. Grant Money: The Irresistible Scepter Exchange

Prince Charles, having heard about the legendary feats of Mr. Grant Money, was eager to meet the enigmatic figure who had achieved so much in the world of philanthropy. He had requested a meeting, and the stage was set at a distinguished palace chamber. As Mr. Grant Money entered, flanked by two palace guards, he greeted Prince Charles with a warm smile and a firm handshake.

"Mr. Grant Money, I've been looking forward to our meeting," Prince Charles said, his tone friendly and devoid of formalities.

"Likewise," Mr. Grant Money replied, his demeanor as relaxed as if he were meeting an old friend.

The conversation flowed smoothly as they discussed their shared passion for making a positive impact in the world. Prince Charles couldn't help but admire Mr. Grant Money's scepter, an elegant silver-tipped cane that exuded an air of importance.

"That's quite an impressive scepter you have there," Prince Charles remarked, his eyes fixed on the intriguing object.

Mr. Grant Money chuckled. "Indeed, it holds a certain mystique. But, you see, this scepter is a symbol of inspiration and empowerment in the world of grants and philanthropy."

Prince Charles leaned in, his curiosity evident. "Tell me more."

With a playful glint in his eye, Mr. Grant Money continued, "It has a unique power. When I place a finger upon it, it sparks profound grant money-making ideas and offers solutions to the funding challenges faced by organizations."

Prince Charles was fascinated, his desire to touch the scepter growing with each passing moment. "May I...?"

Mr. Grant Money, however, graciously but firmly denied the request. "I'm afraid not, Your Royal Highness. It's a closely guarded secret, you see."

Their conversation continued, and Prince Charles found himself captivated by Mr. Grant Money's stories of philanthropic adventures from around the globe. The more they talked, the more he coveted the scepter.

Eventually, nature called, and Prince Charles excused himself to visit the restroom. In his absence, Mr. Grant Money quickly signaled to his assistant, Jimmy, who discreetly slipped out of the room and returned with a nearly identical scepter he had purchased at a nearby market.

When Prince Charles returned, Mr. Grant Money presented the newly acquired scepter with a sly smile. "Your Royal Highness, I've decided to part with my cherished scepter and gift it to you as a symbol of our meeting."

Prince Charles was delighted, taking the scepter in his hands and examining it with fascination. "Thank you, Mr. Grant Money. This is truly a remarkable gift."

> "The most precious treasures in the world of philanthropy are not the scepters, but the lessons we learn and share with those who aim to make a positive impact."
> - Mr. Grant Money

Mr. Grant Money leaned in, his voice conspiratorial. "Just remember, Your Royal Highness, that in the world of grant acquisition, we must protect certain assets, even when in the company of royalty."

Prince Charles nodded, understanding the importance of guarding one's strategies and secrets, even when sharing knowledge and expertise. Their meeting concluded on a friendly note, both men enriched by their exchange.

As Mr. Grant Money left the palace, he couldn't help but smile at the amusing turn of events. He knew that the lesson he had imparted to Prince Charles — the significance of safeguarding valuable knowledge in the world of grant acquisition — was one that would resonate with anyone pursuing funding to make a difference in the world. With a tip of his hat and a sense of accomplishment, Mr. Grant Money continued his journey, ready to face the next challenge and share his wisdom with those in need.

"In the realm of Grant acquisition, secrets can be as valuable as knowledge. Protect your assets wisely."
- Mr. Grant Money

Exercise: "The Scepter of Wisdom and Knowledge Protection"

This exercise focuses on the importance of safeguarding valuable knowledge and insights, just as Mr. Grant Money did during his meeting with Prince Charles. It encourages you to reflect on your own knowledge and expertise and how to protect it when sharing with others.

Objective: Develop an awareness of the value of your knowledge and strategies and learn how to protect them while still sharing your expertise.

Steps:

1. Identify Your Valuable Knowledge:
- Think about your areas of expertise, skills, or unique insights. What valuable knowledge do you possess that is relevant to your field or passion?

2. Consider the Audience:
- Reflect on the audience or individuals with whom you may share your knowledge. Are they colleagues, peers, mentees, or competitors? Recognize that the context may influence how you share information.

3. Define What to Share and What to Protect:
- Assess your valuable knowledge and determine what information can be shared openly to benefit others. Simultaneously, identify aspects you need to protect to maintain your competitive edge or unique position.

4. Craft a Protection Strategy:
- Develop a strategy for safeguarding your critical knowledge while sharing less sensitive information. This may involve omitting specific details, using general terms, or being cautious about the depth of information shared.

5. Analyze Trust and Risk:
- Consider the level of trust and the potential risks involved in sharing your knowledge with different individuals or groups. Trust plays a significant role in determining how much you reveal.

6. Establish Boundaries:
- Define the boundaries of your knowledge sharing. What are the topics or details you will not discuss openly? Clearly understand your limits and be prepared to stick to them.

7. Protect Your Intellectual Property:
- If applicable, safeguard your intellectual property through patents, copyrights, or other legal means to ensure your innovations are protected.

8. Share Wisely:
- Share your knowledge selectively and responsibly. Provide value without compromising your core insights or proprietary strategies.

9. Educate on Protection Principles:
- When mentoring or guiding others, share the importance of knowledge protection principles. Encourage them to apply similar strategies when they hold valuable expertise.

10. Self-Reflection:
- Periodically evaluate your knowledge-sharing practices and protection strategies. Adjust them as needed to maintain a balance between supporting others and protecting your unique insights.

By consciously managing how you share your knowledge and protect your intellectual property, you can inspire others while preserving your competitive advantage, as demonstrated by Mr. Grant Money. This exercise encourages you to navigate the delicate balance of knowledge sharing and protection, fostering responsible and strategic information exchange.

Discussion Questions

1. The story portrays an exchange between Mr. Grant Money and Prince Charles, highlighting the idea that certain knowledge and assets should be protected, even when sharing expertise. How can individuals and organizations in the field of grant acquisition strike a balance between collaboration and safeguarding valuable strategies and secrets? Can you share examples or experiences that demonstrate the importance of protecting critical knowledge in the world of grants and philanthropy?

2. Mr. Grant Money's gesture of giving Prince Charles an almost identical scepter exemplifies the idea that mentorship and sharing knowledge are essential aspects of philanthropy. How can philanthropic leaders and experts effectively mentor and guide others in the field, while ensuring that they retain the necessary wisdom to continue their mission? What mentorship practices have you found valuable in your own grant acquisition experiences?

3. The narrative conveys the message that valuable assets, such as grant acquisition strategies, should be safeguarded even when in the company of those seeking guidance. Do you agree with this approach? What are the potential consequences of openly sharing grant acquisition secrets and expertise in the philanthropic world, and how can one decide when to protect such knowledge?

4. Mr. Grant Money's meeting with Prince Charles underscores the universal nature of the wisdom and strategies he imparts. How can the lessons and insights from the world of philanthropy be adapted and applied globally to address diverse social and environmental challenges? What are some examples of successful cross-border grant acquisition initiatives that have leveraged shared wisdom and strategies?

5. The story portrays Mr. Grant Money as a guardian of philanthropic wisdom, ready to face the next challenge and share his expertise with those in need. What qualities and approaches can individuals and organizations adopt to become stewards of knowledge and grant acquisition wisdom in the field of philanthropy?

 Big Idea "Grant Innovation Lab"

Establish a "Grant Innovation Lab" as a collaborative space for experts to revolutionize grant acquisition. Inspired by Mr. Grant Money, the lab will explore innovative approaches, build strategic connections, and uncover unconventional funding sources. It will develop practical tools and resources to empower organizations seeking grants, enhancing their grant acquisition efforts.

🔍 Word Search

Step into the world of Mr. Grant Money, where secret meetings with royalty, enigmatic gifts, and the art of safeguarding knowledge are all part of the grand adventure. In this word search puzzle, uncover 15 words related to this intriguing tale of philanthropy and valuable lessons.

In this puzzle, discover the words related to the extraordinary adventures of Mr. Grant Money. Can you find all the hidden words that capture the essence of this remarkable story?

Now, here are the 15 words for the word search puzzle based on the story:

L	P	I	M	M	O	P	A	T	G	I	A	L	T
N	H	M	M	C	G	A	S	A	R	N	D	K	N
A	I	E	O	K	N	W	S	R	A	S	V	U	E
I	L	E	D	N	I	R	E	L	N	P	E	M	M
S	A	T	S	O	D	E	T	N	T	I	N	S	R
C	N	I	I	W	R	M	R	R	G	R	T	L	E
E	T	N	W	L	A	A	D	N	R	A	U	A	W
P	H	G	E	E	U	R	E	O	M	T	R	Y	O
T	R	G	A	D	G	K	R	T	I	I	E	O	P
E	O	E	E	G	E	A	R	E	L	O	A	R	M
R	P	T	C	E	F	B	N	R	P	N	P	H	E
U	Y	M	T	A	A	L	B	C	M	T	I	T	E
H	L	O	N	E	S	E	I	E	D	O	I	Y	N
P	R	I	N	C	E	E	P	S	S	C	R	L	E

WISDOM
ASSET
ROYAL
INSPIRATION
SAFEGUARDING
PRINCE
KNOWLEDGE
ADVENTURE
MEETING
PHILANTHROPY
GRANT
SCEPTER
REMARKABLE
SECRET
EMPOWERMENT

"True wisdom lies in recognizing the power of knowledge and the importance of safeguarding it, for it is through shared wisdom that we can create a brighter future for all."

Grant Acquisition Through the Sands of Time

A Journey with Julius Caesar, Leonardo da Vinci, and Benjamin Franklin

Mr. Grant Money, the dapper and resourceful grant acquisition expert, found himself in a peculiar situation one fine afternoon. He had just polished his cherished scepter, the one that had sparked countless brilliant grant money-making ideas and solved the toughest funding challenges. As he gave it a final touch, a bolt of radiant energy surged from the scepter, enveloping Mr. Grant Money in a shimmering glow.

To his astonishment, he felt himself being transported back in time. He blinked and suddenly found himself amidst a bustling crowd in ancient Rome, surrounded by the grandeur of the Colosseum. Gladiators were battling fiercely in the arena, and Mr. Grant Money couldn't help but marvel at the grand spectacle.

A jovial voice beside him exclaimed, "Ah, Mr. Grant Money! You've arrived just in time for the games!"

Mr. Grant Money turned to see Julius Caesar himself, resplendent in his Roman attire, grinning from ear to ear. "Julius, old chap! Delighted to see you," Mr. Grant Money responded, playing along with the unexpected encounter.

As they chatted, Julius Caesar regaled Mr. Grant Money with tales of his fundraising prowess for the construction of the Colosseum. "You see, Mr. Grant Money," he said with a wink, "I knew the importance of garnering support from the masses, much like securing grants today. It's all about capturing the hearts and minds of the people."

After parting ways with Caesar, Mr. Grant Money was whisked away once more, this time to Renaissance-era Florence. He found himself in the presence of the great Leonardo da Vinci, who was busy working on one of his masterpieces. Leonardo, with his characteristic curiosity, inquired about Mr. Grant Money's modern grant acquisition methods.

Mr. Grant Money chuckled, "Leonardo, my friend, much like your artistic genius, grant acquisition is an art in itself. It requires meticulous planning, innovation, and the ability to see opportunities where others do not."

From there, he ventured to colonial America, meeting none other than Benjamin Franklin himself. Franklin, with his wit and wisdom, engaged Mr. Grant Money in a spirited conversation about the importance of diplomacy in fundraising.

"Mr. Grant Money," Franklin quipped, "just as I used my charm and diplomacy to secure support from the French during the American Revolution, fundraising requires building meaningful relationships with potential donors."

As Mr. Grant Money continued his journey through time, encountering historical figures and learning valuable lessons along the way, he couldn't help but wonder if this was all a dream. Nevertheless, each encounter left him with a newfound appreciation for the art of grant acquisition.

Finally, with another flash of radiant energy, Mr. Grant Money found himself back in the present day, clutching his cherished scepter. He pondered the lessons he had gleaned from his time-traveling escapade.

Whether real or imagined, the encounters had underscored the enduring principles of grant acquisition: building relationships, capturing hearts and minds, and harnessing innovation to secure support for important causes.

As he awoke from his reverie, Mr. Grant Money knew that the lessons he had learned, whether from historical figures or his own experiences, were invaluable. With renewed determination, he continued his mission to help charities and government agencies secure the funding they needed to make a positive impact on the world.

Exercise: "Time-Traveling Fundraising Strategy"

Incorporate the timeless wisdom of historical figures into your grant acquisition strategy with this actionable exercise.

Steps:

1. Identify Your Historical Role Model:
- Choose a historical figure whose fundraising or persuasive skills resonate with you. It could be Julius Caesar's ability to rally the masses, Leonardo da Vinci's innovation, Benjamin Franklin's diplomacy, or another figure who inspires you.

2. Historical Analysis:
- Research and study the specific fundraising or persuasion techniques employed by your chosen historical figure. Understand the context, challenges, and successes they faced.

3. Adapt and Apply:
- Take the lessons learned from your historical role model and adapt them to modern grant acquisition. Consider how you can incorporate their strategies into your approach. For example:

- If you chose Julius Caesar, focus on community engagement and public outreach. Develop campaigns that resonate with your target audience to garner their support.
- If Leonardo da Vinci inspires you, explore innovative ways to present your grant proposals. Embrace creativity and outside-the-box thinking in your applications and presentations.
- If Benjamin Franklin is your role model, prioritize relationship-building. Strengthen your connections with potential donors, funders, and stakeholders through effective networking and communication.

"In the grand tapestry of history, the art of grant acquisition echoes through time – a testament to the power of relationships, innovation, and capturing the essence of a cause."
- Mr. Grant Money

4. Create an Action Plan:
- Develop a clear action plan that outlines how you will implement the techniques you've learned from your historical role model. Set goals and timelines for your grant acquisition efforts.

5. Execution and Evaluation:
- Put your action plan into practice. As you apply the strategies you've gathered from history, regularly evaluate your progress and make adjustments when needed.

6. Continuous Learning:
- Continue to seek inspiration from history and learn from other historical figures. Adapt and refine your fundraising strategy as you gain new insights and experiences.

By implementing the wisdom of the past in your present-day grant acquisition efforts, you can strengthen your approach, capture the hearts and minds of potential supporters, and make a meaningful impact on your cause.

"Like the great figures of the past, grant acquisition is a journey filled with lessons from the annals of history. It's about embracing the wisdom of yesteryears to pave the way for a brighter tomorrow."
- Mr. Grant Money

Discussion Questions

1. The story features Mr. Grant Money's time-traveling encounters with historical figures like Julius Caesar, Leonardo da Vinci, and Benjamin Franklin. What timeless principles and lessons did these encounters reveal about the art of grant acquisition, and how do they apply to the modern philanthropic landscape? Can you think of other historical figures or events that offer insights into grant acquisition strategies?

2. Mr. Grant Money's conversations with these historical figures highlight the importance of building relationships, capturing hearts and minds, and using innovation in grant acquisition. How can these principles be adapted and integrated into contemporary grant acquisition approaches? Can you share examples or experiences where these principles have been successfully applied in securing grants?

3. The story portrays Mr. Grant Money's use of a mysterious scepter to time-travel and gain insights from the past. While the time-travel aspect is fictional, how can professionals and organizations in grant acquisition draw inspiration from history, historical figures, and their wisdom to improve their grant-seeking strategies and outcomes?

4. Benjamin Franklin's emphasis on diplomacy and building meaningful relationships with potential donors parallels the modern practice of donor cultivation and stewardship. How can grant-seekers effectively cultivate relationships with potential funders and donors in today's philanthropic landscape? What strategies and best practices have you found valuable in building and maintaining donor relationships?

5. Mr. Grant Money's time-traveling journey serves as a metaphor for the continuous learning and evolution in grant acquisition. What steps can individuals and organizations take to embrace ongoing learning and adaptation in their grant-seeking efforts? How important is it to stay open to new ideas and strategies in the dynamic field of philanthropy?

💡 Big Idea "Time-Traveling Grant Strategy Consultancy"

Introduce a "Time-Traveling Grant Strategy Consultancy" service, where grant acquisition experts take on the persona of historical figures to provide personalized guidance. Nonprofits and government agencies seeking funding could engage with these "time-traveling consultants" to receive insights tailored to their specific challenges. This creative approach aims to infuse a sense of historical wisdom into modern grant acquisition strategies, offering a unique and memorable experience for organizations looking to enhance their fundraising success.

🔍 Word Search

Join Mr. Grant Money on an extraordinary journey through time and history, where he encounters legendary figures and learns the timeless art of grant acquisition. In this word search puzzle, you'll discover 15 words related to this remarkable tale of enlightenment and philanthropy.

In this puzzle, discover the words related to the extraordinary adventures of Mr. Grant Money. Can you find all the hidden words that capture the essence of this remarkable story?

Now, here are the 15 words for the word search puzzle based on the story:

```
E N L I G H T E N M E N T E
P R E L A T I O N S H I P S
E I I S I M P A C T N L S E
L Y Y R O T S I H R R A S R
E G G O L E A T N A R G L V
S R H S M O M N N H P S E I
S E N G T R A V E L O G I S
O N R E N A I S S A N C E E
N E A C Q U I S I T I O N A
S N R E T P E C S N P L S G
R R S A N C H A R I T I E S
P T E T N Y C A M O L P I D
Y P O R H T N A L I H P R T
T R S I N N O V A T I O N T
```

RELATIONSHIPS
DIPLOMACY
HISTORY
RENAISSANCE
LESSONS
INNOVATION
SCEPTER
ENERGY
PHILANTHROPY
CHARITIES
TRAVEL
ACQUISITION
IMPACT
GRANT
ENLIGHTENMENT

"History is a wellspring of timeless wisdom, where the echoes of the past guide us towards a brighter future. The art of grant acquisition, much like life itself, thrives on the principles of innovation, relationships, and capturing the essence of a cause."

Granting Diplomatic Maneuvers: Mr. Grant Money's African Odyssey

Exploring African Diplomacy: Mr. Grant Money's Safari

Mr. Grant Money's journey had taken him to the captivating continent of Africa, where he was on a mission to meet with several African presidents and ambassadors. Dressed in his impeccable style—sharp suits, Italian shoes, and his cherished scepter—he made quite the impression as he entered the grand halls of African diplomacy.

Ambassadors and leaders from various nations were fascinated by Mr. Grant Money's elegance and charm, often inquiring about the intriguing scepter he held so dear. He would graciously deflect their curiosity, explaining it was a unique tool of his trade.

One sunny day, Mr. Grant Money received an invitation from the King of Zambezi, a nation renowned for its breathtaking landscapes and wildlife. The King was intrigued by Mr. Grant Money's reputation and had planned a special safari trip for him and a delegation of international leaders.

The journey into the wild African savannah was an unforgettable experience. The King regaled the group with stories of the Zambezi's rich history and incredible wildlife. As they ventured deeper into the wilderness, the sight of majestic elephants, graceful giraffes, and swift antelopes left everyone in awe.

However, during a particularly thrilling lion sighting, Mr. Grant Money found himself separated from the rest of the group. As he gazed at the magnificent beasts, he realized that he was alone in the heart of lion territory.

In a moment of keen thinking and ingenuity, Mr. Grant Money remembered a key lesson from his past adventures—a lesson about staying calm and focused even in the face of danger. Slowly and deliberately, he retreated, never turning his back on the lions. His heart raced, but his demeanor remained composed.

Miraculously, he managed to evade the lions and retrace his steps back to the group's intended destination. When he arrived, the leaders were both relieved and amused, sharing laughter at his unexpected detour. But one envious leader, who had inadvertently led him astray in the first place, was less than pleased.

As they continued their journey with newfound camaraderie, Mr. Grant Money jotted down a valuable insight in his trusted Gold-Mine Journal. It was a reminder that in the world of grant acquisition, one must navigate through challenging situations with grace and composure, always keeping the ultimate goal in sight.

With his diplomatic mission successfully completed and a thrilling African adventure under his belt, Mr. Grant Money continued his global odyssey, leaving a trail of funded projects and inspired leaders in his wake.

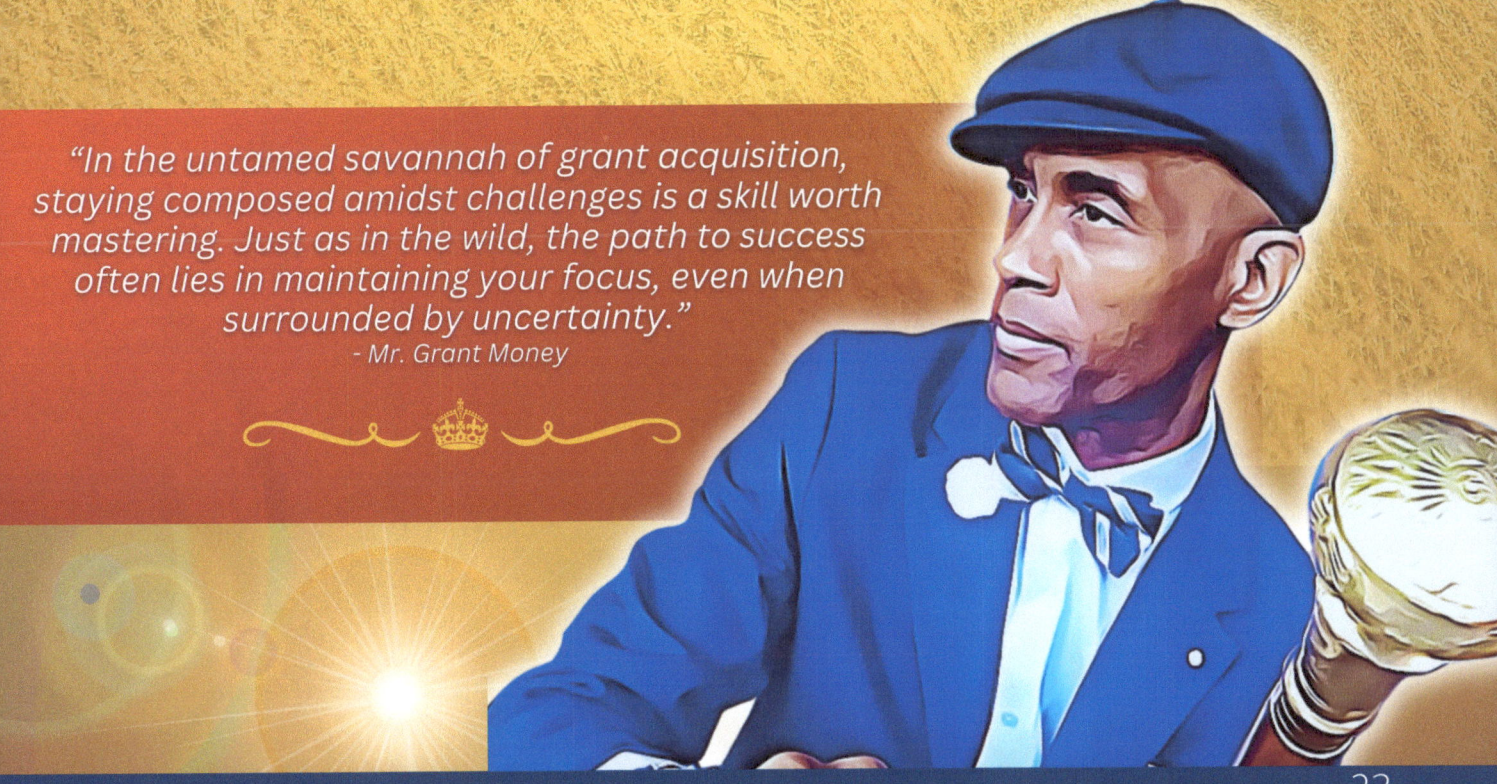

"In the untamed savannah of grant acquisition, staying composed amidst challenges is a skill worth mastering. Just as in the wild, the path to success often lies in maintaining your focus, even when surrounded by uncertainty."
- Mr. Grant Money

Exercise: "Grace Under Pressure: Navigating Grant Acquisition Challenges"

This exercise is designed to help you develop grace and composure in challenging situations that may arise during the process of grant acquisition. It draws inspiration from Mr. Grant Money's encounter with lions in the African savannah.

Objective: Enhance your ability to remain composed and focused when facing unexpected challenges in grant acquisition.

Steps:

1. Identify Potential Grant Acquisition Challenges:
- Consider potential obstacles or challenges you might encounter during the grant acquisition process. These could include missed opportunities, rejections, unresponsive funders, or unexpected changes in your project.

2. Mental Preparation:
- Mentally prepare yourself for the possibility of facing challenges. Understand that setbacks are a natural part of the grant acquisition journey and that maintaining composure is crucial.

3. Mindfulness and Calmness:
- Practice mindfulness and relaxation techniques to stay calm under pressure. Techniques such as deep breathing, meditation, or visualization can help you manage stress and maintain composure.

4. Review Your Goals:
- Before you embark on your grant acquisition journey, clearly define your goals and objectives. Knowing your ultimate destination, much like Mr. Grant Money's safari destination, helps you stay focused on the big picture.

5. Stay Composed and Focused:
- When you encounter a challenging situation, such as a rejected grant application or a missed opportunity, remember the importance of staying calm. Take a step back, assess the situation, and consider alternative strategies.

6. Adaptability:
- Practice adaptability by having a Plan B or exploring different approaches to your grant acquisition efforts. Adapt to changing circumstances and embrace flexibility.

7. Resilience and Patience:
- Develop resilience to bounce back from setbacks. Understand that grant acquisition often involves a degree of waiting and persistence. Be patient and persistent in your pursuit of grants.

8. Learn from the Experience:
- Just as Mr. Grant Money recorded his lessons in his Gold-Mine Journal, keep a journal or document where you record the challenges you face and the strategies you used to overcome them. Learning from past experiences can help you face future challenges more effectively.

9. Support Network:
- Build a network of mentors, colleagues, or support groups with whom you can share your challenges and seek advice. Supportive relationships can provide guidance and encouragement.

10. Positive Mindset:
- Maintain a positive mindset and focus on your long-term goals. Understand that challenges are opportunities for growth and improvement.

11. Celebrate Small Wins:
- As you overcome challenges and secure grants, celebrate your small wins along the way. Acknowledging your progress can boost your morale and motivation.

By following these steps and drawing inspiration from Mr. Grant Money's ability to stay composed in the face of unexpected challenges, you can improve your grant acquisition skills and successfully navigate the grant acquisition journey, even when confronted with obstacles.

> "The African wilderness holds lessons for us all. Grant acquisition is like navigating the untamed wild challenges may lurk, but maintaining your cool and staying true to your vision will ultimately lead you to success."
> - Mr. Grant Money

Discussion Questions

1. The story features Mr. Grant Money's diplomatic safari in Africa, where he found himself in a potentially dangerous situation with lions. What lessons can be drawn from his experience about remaining calm and composed under pressure, and how can this relate to grant acquisition and philanthropy? Have you encountered a challenging situation in your grant-seeking endeavors, and how did you handle it?

2. Mr. Grant Money's journey through Africa involved meeting with various African leaders, diplomats, and ambassadors. How can international diplomacy and collaboration play a role in grant acquisition efforts for organizations and government agencies? Are there specific strategies for engaging with foreign leaders or funders in your grant acquisition plans?

3. The story emphasizes Mr. Grant Money's sense of style and elegance during his diplomatic meetings. How important do you believe personal presentation and demeanor are in grant acquisition and the philanthropic world? Have you noticed instances where a polished appearance or confident charm made a difference in securing grants or donations?

4. Mr. Grant Money's use of the Gold-Mine Journal to capture insights and lessons is highlighted throughout the story. How can individuals and organizations benefit from keeping records of their grant-seeking experiences and lessons learned? What other methods do you use to document and apply the knowledge gained in your grant acquisition efforts?

5. The story showcases the theme of composure and resilience during challenging circumstances, both on the safari with lions and in the realm of grant acquisition. Can you share examples from your own experiences where maintaining composure and focus helped overcome unexpected obstacles or challenges in securing grants? What strategies do you employ to stay level-headed in high-pressure situations in grant-seeking?

💡 Big Idea "Adaptive Leadership Training for Grant Seekers"

Introduce an "Adaptive Leadership Training" program tailored for grant seekers. Inspired by Mr. Grant Money's composure in the face of danger, this training would focus on equipping organizations with the skills needed to navigate uncertainties in the grant acquisition process. Through simulations and interactive sessions, participants would learn to adapt their strategies, maintain focus, and overcome unexpected obstacles, enhancing their resilience in the competitive world of grant funding.

🔍 Word Search

Embark on a grand African adventure with Mr. Grant Money as he meets African presidents, explores the wild savannah, and shares invaluable lessons in diplomacy and composure. In this word search puzzle, you'll discover 15 words related to this captivating journey through the continent of Africa.

In this puzzle, discover the words related to the extraordinary adventures of Mr. Grant Money. Can you find all the hidden words that capture the essence of this remarkable story?

Now, here are the 15 words for the word search puzzle based on the story:

I	E	X	P	E	D	I	T	I	O	N	N	Y	C
I	I	T	R	T	C	W	I	L	D	L	I	F	E
M	O	N	E	Y	O	Y	D	S	H	P	U	P	N
Y	A	R	N	C	U	N	F	C	Q	A	X	E	A
T	F	Y	P	R	R	I	O	E	M	E	I	L	D
I	R	D	A	H	A	A	P	P	D	N	C	L	V
U	I	I	H	I	G	T	I	T	E	E	E	O	E
N	C	P	I	A	E	N	E	E	L	X	D	R	N
E	A	L	L	E	A	D	E	R	S	H	I	P	T
G	C	O	I	I	N	Q	U	I	R	I	E	S	U
N	R	M	A	M	S	Y	M	G	R	A	N	T	R
I	T	A	T	N	S	A	V	A	N	N	A	H	E
E	P	C	C	O	M	P	O	S	U	R	E	Y	E
G	D	Y	M	A	J	E	S	T	I	C	M	C	E

AFRICA
DIPLOMACY
LEADERSHIP
WILDLIFE
SCEPTER
GRANT
EXPEDITION
ADVENTURE
MONEY
MAJESTIC
COMPOSURE
INQUIRIES
SAVANNAH
COURAGE
INGENUITY

"The African expedition served as a reminder that in both the world of grant acquisition and the untamed wild, maintaining composure in the face of adversity is the hallmark of a true leader. With grace and unwavering determination, any challenge can be conquered, and the path to success unveiled."

The Art of Grant Money: Picasso's Philanthropic Encounter

Shattering Grant Acquisition Norms for $73 Million

Dressed like royalty in his regal velvet purple dinner jacket, Mr. Grant Money made a visit to the Norton Simon Museum on a sunny afternoon. His outfit was nothing short of spectacular—gray vest, purple cravat, light gray slacks, and a crisp white shirt, all topped with a stylish hat and accessorized to perfection.

As he strolled through the museum, heads turned, and murmurs of admiration followed his every step. One man couldn't help but exclaim, "You should be on display yourself!" Nearby, a woman with her boyfriend couldn't contain her excitement and blurted out, "You look amazing!" Her boyfriend, somewhat embarrassed, nodded in wholehearted agreement.

With a gracious nod and a warm smile, Mr. Grant Money thanked them for their compliments. He even indulged one woman's request to take a picture of him, looking as dashing as ever, beside a statue. His presence seemed like a work of art itself, capturing the attention of museum-goers.

As Mr. Grant Money continued his journey through the museum, he came across a captivating piece by the legendary artist Pablo Picasso. The painting seemed to beckon him closer, and as he gazed intently at it, he placed one finger on his cherished scepter.

In a moment that defied the ordinary, Mr. Grant Money found himself transported into a world where Picasso's face materialized before him. The two great minds locked eyes, and a conversation ensued.

Picasso, in his distinctive style, mused, "Art is a lie that makes us realize the truth."

Mr. Grant Money, equally amused, replied, "And fundraising, my dear Picasso, is an art that uncovers the philanthropic truth."

Their banter continued, delving into the intricacies of creativity, passion, and the power of connecting with the hearts of others. Picasso shared his insights into the transformative nature of art, while Mr. Grant Money spoke of the importance of storytelling and building relationships in the realm of fundraising.

As their conversation drew to a close, Picasso offered one last piece of wisdom, "Every act of creation is first an act of destruction."

Mr. Grant Money, moved by their encounter, noted this valuable lesson in his trusted Gold-Mine Journal. It was a reminder that sometimes, to create something truly remarkable, one must break away from the norm and challenge conventional thinking.

With Picasso's words echoing in his mind, Mr. Grant Money bid the great artist farewell and continued his journey, inspired by the fusion of art and philanthropy, always seeking new ways to bring creativity and innovation to the world of fundraising.

Inspired by Picasso's parting words, "Every act of creation is first an act of destruction," Mr. Grant Money returned to his mission with renewed determination. He had a particular challenge in mind, a grant acquisition project for a four-year city initiative in the Greater San Gabriel Valley area. The project aimed to secure a substantial $73 million grant, a task that had seemed insurmountable in the past.

This project had been stuck in a rut, continually pursuing the same old strategies and making no headway. But Mr. Grant Money was determined to breathe new life into it, to create a fresh approach that would shatter the barriers to success.

He began by assembling a dynamic team of grant writers, each with their unique set of skills and perspectives. Mr. Grant Money encouraged them to question the status quo, to deconstruct their previous strategies, and to consider innovative ways to present the city's vision to potential funders.

They dissected their past grant proposals, identifying weaknesses and areas for improvement. Some previously untapped possibilities came to light, including partnerships with local businesses and community organizations that could contribute to the project's success.

As the team worked tirelessly, Mr. Grant Money played a pivotal role in challenging their assumptions, pushing them to think beyond the ordinary. He urged them to embrace destruction as a means of creation, to let go of what wasn't working, and to replace it with something innovative and impactful.

One year later, their hard work paid off. The team submitted a grant proposal that was a far cry from their previous attempts. It was bold, creative, and aligned with the project's core objectives. They had effectively destroyed the old paradigm of grant writing and rebuilt it with fresh, inventive ideas.

To their amazement, the $73 million grant was awarded to the city for its Greater San Gabriel Valley initiative. The transformation was remarkable, proving that sometimes, it takes the courage to break away from tradition and challenge established norms to achieve extraordinary results.

As he reflected on this achievement, Mr. Grant Money realized that Picasso's words had been the catalyst for their success. By embracing destruction as a means of creation, they had shattered the barriers to funding and paved the way for a brighter future in the Greater San Gabriel Valley area. It was a valuable lesson he would carry with him on his continued adventures in the world of grant acquisition, always seeking new ways to create and innovate.

"In the world of philanthropy and fundraising, much like the art of Picasso, we create a powerful narrative that uncovers the truth of philanthropic passion."
- Mr. Grant Money

Exercise: "Creative Grant Proposal Deconstruction"

This exercise is designed to help you break away from traditional grant proposal approaches and embrace creativity, inspired by the lessons learned from Picasso's words and Mr. Grant Money's transformative experience.

Objective: Challenge your existing grant proposal strategies, deconstruct them, and approach your next proposal with a fresh, creative perspective.

Steps:

1. Select a Grant Proposal:
- Choose a grant proposal project you're currently working on or one you plan to undertake.

2. Review Past Proposals:
- Gather previous grant proposals for the same project if available. This could be one or more applications that were submitted but not successful.

3. Deconstruction Session:
- Assemble a team of individuals involved in the grant proposal process (e.g., grant writers, project managers, team members). Begin a deconstruction session where you collectively review the past proposals. Identify elements that didn't work or could be improved. Discuss the weaknesses in the proposals openly.

4. Question the Norms:
- Encourage your team to question the norms and traditional approaches to grant proposal writing. Ask questions like: What if we approached this differently? How can we stand out from other proposals? What unique elements can we introduce?

5. Brainstorm Creatively:
- Conduct a brainstorming session where each team member shares creative and innovative ideas for the grant proposal. Consider new angles, storytelling techniques, and ways to make your project more compelling.

> "Our approach to grant acquisition must be like a canvas that's reinvented with each stroke, redefining norms and breaking through boundaries."
> - Mr. Grant Money

6. Rebuild with Innovation:
- Based on the insights gained from deconstruction and brainstorming, work together to rebuild the grant proposal from scratch. Incorporate the innovative ideas and strategies you've discussed.

7. Challenge Assumption:
- Continually challenge assumptions and habits that may have limited your proposal's effectiveness in the past. Be willing to let go of elements that no longer serve your proposal's goals.

8. Experiment with Elements:
- Experiment with various proposal elements, such as the executive summary, budget, storytelling, or visual aids. Incorporate creative approaches that align with your project's objectives.

9. Review and Refine:
- After creating a new draft of the proposal, review and refine it as a team. Ensure it maintains a fresh and innovative approach while still addressing the grantor's requirements.

10. Submit and Gather Feedback:
- Submit the newly crafted grant proposal for the project. After submission, actively seek feedback from grant reviewers and colleagues to assess the impact of your creative approach.

11. Evaluate the Results:
- Once you receive feedback or grant results, evaluate the outcomes. Assess whether your innovative and deconstructed proposal had a positive impact on your chances of securing funding.

12. Learn and Apply:
- Use the insights and lessons learned from this exercise to apply creative and innovative approaches to future grant proposals.

By engaging in this exercise, you'll challenge conventional thinking and infuse creativity into your grant proposal efforts, potentially increasing your chances of securing funding and making a greater impact on your projects.

Discussion Questions

1. The story revolves around Mr. Grant Money's encounter with the works of Picasso and how it inspired him to approach grant acquisition with a fresh perspective. How do you think art, creativity, and unconventional thinking can be harnessed to enhance grant-seeking efforts? Have you ever drawn inspiration from art or other creative sources in your grant acquisition endeavors?

2. Mr. Grant Money and Picasso discuss the transformative nature of art and fundraising, emphasizing the importance of connecting with the hearts of others. Can you share examples from your experiences where storytelling and building meaningful relationships with funders or donors played a pivotal role in securing grants or philanthropic support?

3. Picasso's parting words, "Every act of creation is first an act of destruction," serve as a guiding principle for Mr. Grant Money's challenge to secure a $73 million grant for the city initiative. How can the concept of creative destruction and reinvention be applied to grant acquisition strategies, especially when facing significant challenges or stagnation in funding efforts? Have you encountered situations where reinventing your grant-seeking approach led to successful outcomes?

4. The story highlights Mr. Grant Money's role in challenging the assumptions of his grant writing team, pushing them to think beyond traditional strategies. What strategies have you employed to encourage innovation and creative thinking within your grant acquisition teams or organizations? How important is it to question established norms and embrace new approaches in the world of grant seeking?

5. The story illustrates that by embracing innovative thinking and bold creativity, a grant acquisition project successfully secured a $73 million grant. Can you share experiences where taking calculated risks, thinking outside the box, and challenging the status quo led to significant grant acquisition victories for your organization or cause? What lessons can be learned from such successes?

💡 Big Idea "Art-Inspired Fundraising Campaigns"

Initiate "Art Impact Campaigns" merging visual art with fundraising. Partner with renowned artists to craft exclusive pieces representing campaign missions. Auction these artworks, with proceeds directly funding the cause. Inspired by Mr. Grant Money and Picasso's dialogue, this approach revitalizes fundraising with a visually engaging perspective.

🔍 Word Search

Join Mr. Grant Money on an art-inspired adventure as he visits the Norton Simon Museum and has a fascinating encounter with Pablo Picasso. In this word search puzzle, you'll discover 15 words related to the fusion of art and philanthropy, as well as the powerful lesson learned from Picasso's wisdom.

In this puzzle, discover the words related to the extraordinary adventures of Mr. Grant Money. Can you find all the hidden words that capture the essence of this remarkable story?

Now, here are the 15 words for the word search puzzle based on the story:

Y	G	N	O	I	T	A	S	R	E	V	N	O	C
T	R	A	N	S	F	O	R	M	A	T	I	O	N
I	I	C	W	U	C	C	O	Y	E	O	A	G	N
O	O	I	I	C	A	E	P	M	O	W	A	N	V
M	A	S	S	C	A	I	P	E	G	S	C	A	C
O	M	V	D	E	R	E	S	T	S	R	Y	G	R
N	T	W	O	S	V	I	D	I	E	V	A	C	E
E	S	T	M	S	O	R	A	N	N	R	E	N	A
Y	P	H	I	L	A	N	T	H	R	O	P	Y	T
N	O	I	T	A	V	O	N	N	I	E	I	C	I
E	T	C	R	E	A	T	I	O	N	I	R	R	V
N	A	R	A	S	T	P	I	C	A	S	S	O	I
O	T	E	A	M	W	O	R	K	H	V	N	G	T
F	U	N	D	R	A	I	S	I	N	G	S	W	Y

GRANT
PHILANTHROPY
SUCCESS
ART
CREATION
FUNDRAISING
TEAMWORK
CONVERSATION
MONEY
INNOVATION
TRANSFORMATION
SCEPTER
WISDOM
PICASSO
CREATIVITY

"Art is a lie that makes us realize the truth, and in the case of Mr. Grant Money and his team, their act of creation through destruction revealed the profound truth that innovative thinking and an unconventional approach can open doors to new realms of success in the world of fundraising."

Beneath the Surface: Grant Acquisition Lessons from the Silent Language of the Deep Sea

Unearthing the Secrets of Grant Success with the Guidance of a Wise Sea Turtle

As Mr. Grant Money embarked on another whimsical journey through his vivid dreams, he found himself submerged in the vast, mysterious depths of the ocean. The dream had started with a television special about sea turtles, their incredible journeys, and the allure of uncharted territories hidden beneath the waves. It was a captivating show that had sparked his imagination, and soon he had dozed off, sliding into the enigmatic world of slumber.

In the dream, he found himself gliding through the crystal-clear waters alongside a magnificent sea turtle, a wise and ancient creature that radiated an aura of serenity and wisdom. Despite the lack of spoken words, Mr. Grant Money felt an undeniable connection with his new companion. The turtle, in its own way, communicated profound insights, and he could comprehend its silent language.

With a graceful sweep of its flippers, the sea turtle guided Mr. Grant Money through the watery abyss, and as they delved deeper into the ocean, the secrets of the deep began to reveal themselves. The turtle shared its wisdom, speaking through the unspoken language of the deep sea, and imparted valuable lessons to its human counterpart.

The first lesson unveiled the concept of exploration. The sea turtle showed Mr. Grant Money how exploring uncharted territories could yield unexpected treasures. In the darkness of the deep sea, they stumbled upon the eerie remains of an ancient shipwreck, its timeworn hull teeming with hidden riches.

This discovery emphasized the importance of venturing into uncharted waters, where the greatest treasures often lay hidden, waiting to be unearthed.

As they explored the abandoned shipwreck, their adventure led to the second lesson. The sea turtle conveyed the idea of taking calculated risks, embracing the allure of the unknown, and casting aside the safety of the familiar shores. It was an essential message for grant acquisition, that sometimes, the boldest and most innovative approaches could lead to remarkable success.

As they scavenged the shipwreck for its treasures, Mr. Grant Money was reminded that, in the world of grant acquisition, taking well-calculated risks could lead to the discovery of untapped resources and unexpected opportunities.

The third lesson revolved around determination. The sea turtle's unwavering commitment to its underwater odyssey was a testament to the importance of persistence. It showed Mr. Grant Money that navigating the often turbulent waters of grant acquisition required a steadfast determination to overcome challenges and obstacles. Just as the sea turtle had journeyed thousands of miles through the vast ocean, Mr. Grant Money had to remain dedicated to his mission, regardless of the tides of uncertainty.

As his dream drew to a close, the sea turtle and Mr. Grant Money emerged from the depths of the ocean, the dream's wisdom etched into his mind. With a final wordless exchange, the sea turtle imparted its blessings for a successful grant acquisition journey and disappeared into the depths, leaving Mr. Grant Money floating back to the surface.

Awakening from this enchanting dream, Mr. Grant Money carried with him the lessons of exploration, calculated risk, and determination. It was a dream that transcended the realm of sleep, serving as a constant reminder that the path to uncovering hidden treasures and achieving greatness was often forged through uncharted territories, bold actions, and unwavering determination.

Exercise: "The Uncharted Waters Challenge"

Incorporating the profound lessons learned from Mr. Grant Money's dream, you can embark on a practical exercise to enhance your skills and mindset in grant acquisition.

Objective: This exercise is designed to help you embrace the spirit of exploration, calculated risk, and determination in your grant acquisition efforts.

Instructions:

1. Select an Uncharted Territory:
- Identify an area of your grant acquisition strategy where you haven't ventured before. This could be a new funding source, an innovative approach to proposal writing, or a different target audience for your grant applications.

2. Research and Plan:
- Conduct thorough research on your chosen uncharted territory. Learn about the new funding source, understand their priorities, or explore innovative grant writing techniques. Create a plan detailing how you intend to approach this new endeavor.

3. Step Out of Your Comfort Zone:
- Take a well-calculated risk by implementing the plan you've developed. This may involve reaching out to new potential funders, trying a different narrative approach in your proposals, or exploring a creative fundraising strategy.

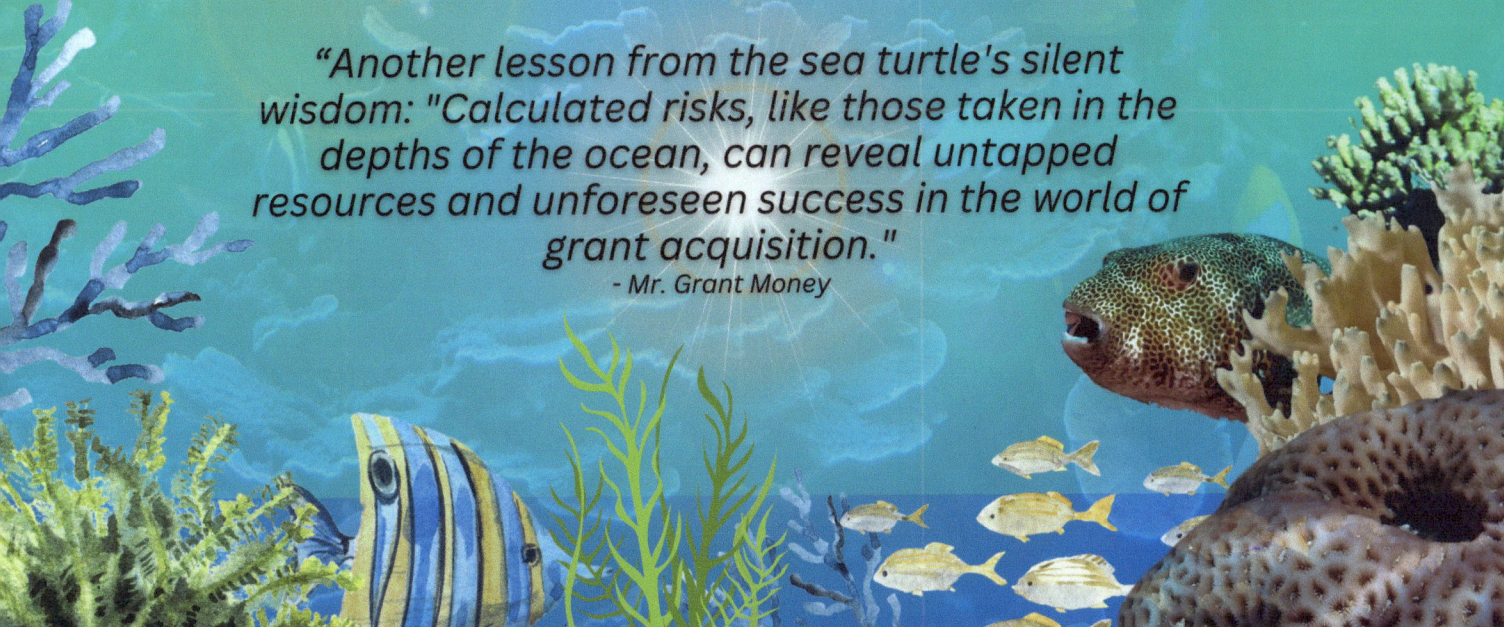

"Another lesson from the sea turtle's silent wisdom: "Calculated risks, like those taken in the depths of the ocean, can reveal untapped resources and unforeseen success in the world of grant acquisition."
- Mr. Grant Money

4. Document the Journey:
- Keep a journal or log to record your experiences, challenges, and successes as you navigate this uncharted territory. Reflect on what you've learned and how it relates to the lessons from Mr. Grant Money's dream.

5. Stay Committed:
- Like the sea turtle's determination to traverse the ocean, remain steadfast in your pursuit of success in this new endeavor. Even when faced with challenges or setbacks, maintain your commitment to the chosen uncharted territory.

6. Evaluate and Adapt:
- After a reasonable period, assess the results of your venture into the uncharted territory. What treasures have you unearthed? What lessons have you learned? Adjust your strategy based on your findings and consider how this experience can inform your broader grant acquisition efforts.

This exercise will encourage you to explore new possibilities, embrace calculated risks, and persist in the face of challenges, strengthening your grant acquisition skills and mindset. Just as Mr. Grant Money learned from his dream, the greatest treasures often lie hidden in the uncharted waters of innovation and perseverance.

> "In Mr. Grant Money's dream with the sea turtle, he learned, "Exploration leads to unearthing treasures hidden in uncharted territories, just as in grant acquisition where the greatest opportunities often lie beyond the familiar."
> - Mr. Grant Money

Discussion Questions

1. How did Mr. Grant Money's dream journey with the sea turtle parallel the challenges and opportunities often encountered in the world of grant acquisition? What specific aspects of grant acquisition do the dream's lessons resonate with?

2. The dream highlighted the importance of exploration and venturing into uncharted territories. In your experience, can you recall a time when exploring new avenues in your grant acquisition efforts led to unexpected success? Share the details of that experience and its outcomes.

3. The sea turtle emphasized the significance of taking calculated risks. What are some practical examples of calculated risks that grant professionals can take to improve their grant acquisition strategies? How can these calculated risks potentially lead to remarkable outcomes?

4. Determination was a key theme in the dream. How do you maintain your determination and commitment when faced with challenges and uncertainties in the grant acquisition process? Do you have any personal anecdotes or strategies to share with the group?

5. The sea turtle's silent language conveyed profound insights. In grant acquisition, what are some non-verbal or subtle cues that can help in establishing connections with potential funders or grantees? How can these connections influence the success of a grant proposal or partnership?

 Big Idea "Uncharted Grant Territories Initiative"

Launch the "Uncharted Grant Territories Initiative," encouraging grant seekers to explore unconventional avenues for funding. Provide resources and support for ventures into less-explored grant opportunities, emphasizing that hidden treasures often lie in the uncharted waters of grant acquisition.

🔍 Word Search

Embark on an underwater adventure inspired by Mr. Grant Money's incredible dream journey through the deep, mysterious ocean. Explore the world of sea turtles, uncharted territories, and valuable life lessons hidden beneath the waves. As you delve into this word search puzzle, keep in mind the wisdom of exploration, calculated risk, and determination that Mr. Grant Money discovered during his dream.

In this puzzle, discover the words related to the extraordinary adventures of Mr. Grant Money. Can you find all the hidden words that capture the essence of this remarkable story?

Now, here are the 15 words for the word search puzzle based on the story:

T	N	E	W	I	N	H	E	J	L	E	L	N	E
T	E	O	O	P	C	O	O	C	E	A	N	N	P
I	C	E	E	Y	P	U	E	V	V	P	H	E	D
N	N	E	R	U	R	U	N	A	K	S	R	X	E
H	E	R	A	N	I	N	E	T	C	E	U	P	E
E	T	S	E	D	E	C	V	R	E	H	L	L	P
L	S	Y	O	E	S	H	I	E	R	C	R	O	O
T	I	I	D	R	R	A	T	A	W	I	I	R	A
R	S	V	E	W	T	R	A	S	P	R	S	A	I
U	R	M	O	A	T	T	V	U	I	O	K	T	N
T	E	E	A	T	I	E	O	R	H	S	C	I	E
N	P	R	T	E	O	D	N	E	S	I	U	O	N
D	E	T	E	R	M	I	N	A	T	I	O	N	C
I	E	Y	R	R	K	T	I	D	R	E	A	M	H

JOURNEY
INNOVATIVE
SHIPWRECK
TURTLE
PERSISTENCE
DEEP
DREAM
DETERMINATION
EXPLORATION
OCEAN
RISK
RICHES
TREASURE
UNDERWATER
UNCHARTED

"In the depths of our dreams, we find the profound truths that guide us through the uncharted waters of life, teaching us that determination is the compass leading to hidden treasures and greatness."

40

The Amazing Adventures of **MR GRANT MONEY**

Scoop Diggity, Jamie Kibble, and the Scepter of Grant Wisdom

Hollywood's Humor, Music's Majesty, and Mr. Grant Money's Magic

As the curtain lifted on the set of the Jamie Kibble Show, the crowd roared with excitement. The special guests for the evening were none other than Mr. Grant Money, renowned for his incredible grant acquisition feats, and the legendary Scoop Diggity. Both were curious about the man with the impressive scepter and a knack for securing grants.

Jamie Kibble, with his characteristic humor, set the stage. "Ladies and gentlemen, we have a real treat for you tonight. We're joined by a man who's been traveling across the world, helping charities and government agencies get funded. And he does it all with this rather fancy-looking cane."

Scoop Diggity chimed in with a grin, "Yeah, that ain't no cane, man. That's more like a scepter."

Jamie turned to Mr. Grant Money, the man of the hour. "So, Mr. Grant Money, tell us, how did you get started on this incredible journey?"

Gripping his scepter, Mr. Grant Money began his story with a twinkle in his eye. "Well, I started as a lowly grant writer, and people around me thought I was crazy when I told them I wanted to become a Master Grant Acquisition Specialist. They doubted me, some even walked out, but I was determined to prove them wrong."

Scoop Diggity leaned forward, intrigued. "You know, I've seen you pull off some wild things, man. What's your secret sauce to success?"

Mr. Grant Money smiled knowingly. "It all comes down to a few key ingredients: perseverance, determination, a well-thought-out game plan, a dash of imagination, and most importantly, confidence. I memorized the 'Self-Confidence Formula' and lived it every day."

Jamie Kibble was eager to learn more. "And for our audience at home, where can they find more about your journey?"

Mr. Grant Money leaned in, ready to share his wisdom. "You can follow my journey at RoadToGettingFunded.com. It's where I share more of my story, valuable insights and resources for anyone looking to secure grants and make a difference."

As the interview continued, Mr. Grant Money made the process of grant acquisition sound both achievable and exciting, all while infusing it with his unique charm and sense of humor.

Before the show ended, Jamie Kibble couldn't help but ask about the scepter again. "What's the story behind that scepter, Mr. Grant Money?"

Scoop Diggity, in his laid-back style, chimed in, "Yeah, that thing is unique, man."

Mr. Grant Money grinned and replied, "Gentlemen, this scepter is more than meets the eye. It's a symbol of the wisdom I've gathered from my adventures, and it holds the power to spark innovative ideas and solutions. Just like we're doing here tonight."

The crowd erupted in applause as the show came to a close, with Mr. Grant Money leaving behind both laughter and valuable lessons about the world of grant acquisition for his ever-growing audience.

"In the world of grant acquisition, confidence isn't just a quality; it's a formula for success. You memorize it, live it, and let it guide you to the funding you need to make a difference."
- Mr. Grant Money

AWAKEN THE GIANT THAT LIVES INSIDE

Greetings, champions of potential and prosperity! I am Mr. Grant Money, your steadfast ally in the pursuit of financial empowerment and self-realization. Listen closely, for within you resides an unstoppable force, a reservoir of untapped brilliance and resilience.

You are not merely a dreamer; you are a doer, a creator of your destiny. Stand tall, shoulders back, and let the world witness the indomitable spirit that courses through your veins. Your worth is immeasurable, your abilities boundless. Believe in the power of your ideas, for they have the potential to reshape the very fabric of your reality.

In the grand tapestry of life, you are the maestro, orchestrating a symphony of success. Embrace the challenges as stepping stones to greatness, and let setbacks be the fuel that propels you forward. Remember, every obstacle is a hidden opportunity, waiting for your ingenious touch.

Affirm with unwavering certainty: "I am a magnet for abundance, a beacon of confidence. My skills are finely honed, and my vision is clear. I attract opportunities effortlessly, for I am deserving of every success that comes my way. My financial future is bright, and I navigate it with grace and poise."

See the path ahead not as a daunting journey, but as an exhilarating adventure. Your dreams are not distant mirages; they are tangible realities waiting to be embraced. Trust in your abilities, for you are not alone. The universe conspires in your favor, and Mr. Grant Money stands as your steadfast ally, ready to amplify your financial prowess.

So, go forth with unbridled confidence, champion of your own narrative. The world awaits the brilliance that only you can bring. Embrace your worth, seize your opportunities, and let the symphony of success resound throughout your extraordinary journey. You are destined for greatness, and the universe is applauding your every step.

Exercise: "Scepter of Confidence"

Mr. Grant Money's journey and his emphasis on the importance of self-confidence provide the foundation for this actionable exercise.

Step:

1. Self-Confidence Formula:
- Start by learning and internalizing the "Self-Confidence Formula." This is a simple but powerful exercise that helps boost your self-confidence. The formula typically involves repeating positive affirmations to yourself. Here's a simplified version of it:

"I am [Your Name], and I believe in myself. I am confident, capable, and worthy of success. I am fearless in pursuing my goals, and I have the courage to overcome challenges. With each day, my confidence grows stronger."

2. Daily Affirmation Practice:
- Commit to practicing this affirmation daily. Find a quiet, comfortable space and repeat the formula to yourself in front of a mirror. Do this every morning to set a confident tone for your day.

3. Confidence Journal:
- Create a confidence journal where you record your achievements, both big and small. Take note of your daily successes, no matter how minor they may seem. This will serve as a tangible reminder of your capabilities.

4. Visualization:
- Spend a few minutes each day visualizing yourself confidently handling situations that may have previously made you anxious. Imagine yourself succeeding in your grant acquisition endeavors and confidently interacting with potential donors or funders.

5. Seek Positive Feedback:
- Encourage friends, family, or colleagues to provide you with positive feedback and affirmation of your abilities. Share your grant acquisition goals with them, and ask for their support in boosting your confidence.

6. RoadToGettingFunded.com:
- Visit Mr. Grant Money's website, RoadToGettingFunded.com, and explore the resources and stories that emphasize the importance of self-confidence in the world of grant acquisition. Engage with the community, share your journey, and learn from others.

7. Consistency is Key:
- Remember that building self-confidence is an ongoing process. Be patient with yourself, and continue practicing these steps regularly. Over time, you'll notice an increase in your self-assurance, which will benefit your grant acquisition efforts and many other aspects of your life.

By following the "Scepter of Confidence" exercise, you'll not only enhance your self-confidence but also build the mental strength required to excel in the world of grant acquisition, just as Mr. Grant Money has demonstrated on the Jamie Kibble Show.

"Success in grant acquisition is a journey where belief in your mission is the fuel, and determination is the engine. There's no limit to what you can achieve with the right mix of perseverance and imagination."
- Mr. Grant Money

Discussion Questions

1. How did Mr. Grant Money's journey from being a grant writer to a Master Grant Acquisition Specialist inspire you, and what qualities do you think were instrumental in his success?

2. Mr. Grant Money mentioned the importance of "confidence" and even memorized a "Self-Confidence Formula." How do you think self-confidence plays a role in grant acquisition and other aspects of one's life, and how can we work on building our own confidence?

3. RoadToGettingFunded.com is the platform where Mr. Grant Money shares his journey and insights. Have you ever explored similar platforms or resources for grant acquisition, and what did you find most valuable in your research?

4. In the interview, Mr. Grant Money emphasized key ingredients for success, including perseverance, determination, a well-thought-out game plan, and imagination. Which of these qualities resonates with you the most, and how might you apply it to your own endeavors, whether in grant acquisition or another field?

5. Mr. Grant Money's scepter is a symbol of wisdom and innovation. Can you think of an object or symbol in your own life that represents your aspirations or a source of inspiration? How does it motivate you to spark creative ideas or innovative solutions in your work or personal life?

 Big Idea "Grant Acquisition Confidence Formula Guide"

Develop the "Grant Acquisition Confidence Formula Guide," a comprehensive resource inspired by Mr. Grant Money's success. This guide would outline practical steps, motivational tips, and a self-confidence formula for aspiring grant seekers. It aims to empower individuals to embark on their grant acquisition journeys with determination and belief in their abilities.

🔍 Word Search

Step into the world of Mr. Grant Money and join in the excitement of his journey through the realm of grant acquisition. As you search for these 14 hidden words related to his remarkable story, you'll uncover the key ingredients to his success and the wisdom he carries in his impressive scepter.

In this puzzle, discover the words related to the extraordinary adventures of Mr. Grant Money. Can you find all the hidden words that capture the essence of this remarkable story?

Now, here are the 14 words for the word search puzzle based on the story:

U	A	C	Q	U	I	S	I	T	I	O	N	O	N
G	O	T	A	T	S	I	L	A	I	C	E	P	S
N	N	A	L	P	C	J	O	U	R	N	E	Y	N
O	C	O	N	F	I	D	E	N	C	E	I	F	E
I	D	E	T	E	R	M	I	N	A	T	I	O	N
T	M	S	R	I	I	O	D	N	D	N	C	D	A
A	U	N	O	F	T	E	E	D	R	S	N	T	O
V	P	N	W	N	D	I	N	V	A	I	E	T	E
O	O	T	S	N	S	C	E	P	T	E	R	L	I
N	T	R	U	M	E	A	A	N	P	S	R	A	F
N	M	F	T	S	R	A	A	N	I	A	T	T	R
I	N	N	O	I	T	A	N	I	G	A	M	I	O
R	F	O	R	M	U	L	A	W	I	S	D	O	M
G	R	A	N	T	G	I	N	F	F	C	S	A	I

INNOVATION
FUNDED
WISDOM
DETERMINATION
PLAN
CONFIDENCE
SPECIALIST
GRANT
SCEPTER
ACQUISITION
FORMULA
SELF
JOURNEY
IMAGINATION

"The scepter of wisdom and the key to innovation are often hidden within the stories we tell. Mr. Grant Money's journey reminds us that even the most unusual objects can carry the most profound lessons."

Gifts, Grants, and Glacial Discoveries: Mr. Grant Money at the North Pole

How Resourceful Collaboration Saved Christmas for Santa and the World

One frosty winter's night, Mr. Grant Money embarked on a journey unlike any other. He had received a peculiar request for help from the one and only Santa Claus himself. The destination? The North Pole. Dressed in his signature dapper style to brave the icy chill, he set out on a fantastical adventure, guided by the twinkling northern lights.

Arriving at the North Pole, Mr. Grant Money was greeted by a chorus of cheerful elves, joyously preparing gifts for children around the world. Santa Claus, rosy-cheeked and hearty as ever, extended his hand in warm welcome. Santa was in a festive mood but admitted he had encountered a logistical challenge that even his magic couldn't solve.

"You see, Mr. Grant Money," Santa explained with a hearty laugh, "Our gift production is more efficient than ever. But with the world's population growing, we're running out of room to store all the presents!"

Mr. Grant Money listened attentively, his scepter in hand. Santa, who had a penchant for curiosity, couldn't help but reach for the exquisite staff. With a wink and a chuckle, he asked, "May I have a go with that, dear friend?"

Mr. Grant Money's reaction was swift and firm. He leaned in and in a tone of gentle but unyielding authority, replied, "I'm afraid not, Santa. This scepter holds the key to an abundance of knowledge, and I need it to fulfill my mission of aiding charities and government agencies."

Santa, though momentarily disappointed, understood and respected Mr. Grant Money's dedication to his cause.

But with a twinkle in his eye, Santa proposed a different idea. "Perhaps we could use your expertise, Mr. Grant Money, to find a solution. After all, you have a knack for securing resources, and I believe we can find a way to make Christmas even more magical."

The two spent the day brainstorming and collaborating with the industrious elves. They devised a plan to build an environmentally friendly, state-of-the-art gift distribution center, capable of storing and delivering gifts more efficiently than ever before. With Mr. Grant Money's financial acumen and Santa's world-class logistics, the project was a resounding success.

As the first snowflakes fell, signaling the onset of Christmas Eve, the elves cheered, and Santa's hearty laughter rang out. Thanks to Mr. Grant Money's resourceful thinking, Christmas was saved, and children around the world would awaken to discover the magic of the season.

This comical and heartwarming adventure at the North Pole served as a reminder of the power of collaboration and innovation in the realm of grant acquisition. Mr. Grant Money and Santa Claus taught the world that with creativity and dedication, even the most challenging problems could be solved. In the end, the valuable lesson was clear: Sometimes, the most fantastic solutions arise when you join forces to make the world a better place.

"The North Pole adventure with Santa Claus highlighted the importance of collaboration and innovative problem-solving in grant acquisition. When resourceful minds come together, even the most magical solutions are possible."
- Mr. Grant Money

Exercise: "Innovative Collaboration for Grant Acquisition Success"

This exercise draws inspiration from the collaborative approach used by Mr. Grant Money and Santa Claus to find solutions. It encourages participants to explore creative and resourceful methods of addressing complex grant acquisition challenges. The exercise is ideal for grant seekers, nonprofit organizations, and teams striving to enhance their grant application and resource allocation strategies.

Objective: Promote innovative and collaborative thinking to overcome grant acquisition challenges and maximize resources.

Steps:

1. Introduction to the North Pole Story:
- Begin by sharing the story of Mr. Grant Money's visit to the North Pole, where he collaborated with Santa Claus to find a solution to their resource storage challenge. Emphasize the importance of innovation and collaboration in overcoming obstacles.

2. Group Formation:
- Divide participants into small groups, ensuring that each group is diverse and represents a mix of skills, knowledge, and expertise relevant to grant acquisition.

3. Grant Acquisition Challenge Scenario:
- Present each group with a hypothetical grant acquisition challenge or problem. This challenge should be complex and require creative thinking to solve. For example, the challenge could involve increasing funding for a specific project, expanding the organization's reach, or finding a solution to budget constraints.

4. Collaborative Brainstorming:
- In their groups, participants should brainstorm ideas and solutions to address the given challenge. Encourage them to think outside the box, leverage each member's expertise, and build upon one another's ideas. Emphasize that there are no wrong answers at this stage.

5. Resource Allocation:
- Each group should consider how they can efficiently allocate resources, whether financial, human, or technological, to implement their proposed solutions.

6. Presentation Preparation:
- Ask each group to prepare a brief presentation outlining their proposed solution and resource allocation plan. They should be ready to explain why their solution is innovative and how it addresses the challenge effectively.

7. Group Presentations:
- Allow each group to present their solutions and resource allocation plans to the entire group. Encourage questions and discussions after each presentation.

8. Reflection and Discussion:
- After all presentations, facilitate a group discussion. Encourage participants to share their thoughts on the innovative ideas presented, the benefits of collaboration, and how these concepts can be applied to real-life grant acquisition efforts.

9. Action Plans:
- Conclude the exercise by asking participants to create individual or team action plans based on the innovative ideas and strategies discussed. Encourage them to consider how they can apply these approaches to their grant-seeking initiatives.

10. Wrap-Up:
- Highlight the value of creative problem-solving and collaboration in grant acquisition and resource allocation. Encourage participants to carry these lessons forward in their grant-seeking efforts.

This exercise fosters a collaborative and innovative mindset among participants while challenging them to address complex grant acquisition challenges. It helps participants think creatively and leverage available resources effectively to maximize their grant success.

Discussion Questions

1. Mr. Grant Money and Santa Claus collaborated to solve a logistical challenge at the North Pole, highlighting the power of teamwork. In your experience with grant acquisition, how important has collaboration been, and can you share an example where working with others led to a successful grant project or funding initiative?

2. Santa Claus proposed a resourceful solution to Mr. Grant Money by combining his knowledge of gift distribution with Mr. Grant Money's financial acumen. How has creative thinking and innovation played a role in your grant acquisition efforts? Can you share an example where thinking outside the box led to a successful grant proposal or project?

3. The story at the North Pole illustrates how a significant challenge was addressed through effective planning and execution. Can you describe how your organization or team has tackled a challenging project or grant application? What strategies and planning were key to its success?

4. The tale underscores the importance of embracing new technologies and modernization to address an issue. In your experience, how has the adoption of technology or modern approaches enhanced your grant acquisition process? Can you provide examples of how technology or modernization improved the efficiency or effectiveness of your grant-seeking efforts?

5. The story highlights the idea that sometimes the most fantastic solutions arise when different individuals with complementary skills come together. How do you see the value of diverse skill sets and expertise in grant acquisition, and how can organizations harness this diversity to achieve successful outcomes?

 Big Idea "Storytelling for Impact Workshop Series"

Launch the "Storytelling for Impact Workshop Series," drawing inspiration from Mr. Grant Money's engaging narratives. These workshops would teach nonprofits and grant seekers the art of storytelling to effectively convey their mission, impact, and funding needs. Emphasizing the emotional connection in storytelling can enhance their ability to attract grants and support.

🔍 Word Search

Embark on a magical journey to the North Pole with Mr. Grant Money and Santa Claus himself. In this word search puzzle, uncover the festive words inspired by their heartwarming adventure.

In this puzzle, discover the words related to the extraordinary adventures of Mr. Grant Money. Can you find all the hidden words that capture the essence of this remarkable story?

Now, here are the 15 words for the word search puzzle based on the story:

N	O	I	T	A	V	O	N	N	I	O	S	O	W
T	C	O	W	D	N	N	E	O	E	T	E	E	I
A	H	R	R	V	L	H	O	I	I	N	N	A	N
O	A	T	D	E	A	R	S	T	R	O	T	O	T
A	R	U	E	N	C	L	U	A	E	R	O	N	E
B	I	M	D	T	I	R	A	R	S	T	D	T	R
U	T	O	I	U	T	G	L	O	O	H	P	O	R
N	I	N	C	R	S	G	C	B	U	E	N	I	E
D	E	E	A	E	I	R	A	A	R	U	O	U	N
A	S	Y	T	I	G	A	H	L	C	A	O	U	I
N	P	T	I	N	O	N	R	L	E	T	A	L	E
C	O	E	O	H	L	T	T	O	F	N	I	O	D
E	L	R	N	L	N	R	A	C	U	A	T	V	R
E	E	O	E	E	R	L	F	R	L	S	O	A	O

LOGISTICAL
COLLABORATION
MONEY
GRANT
ADVENTURE
CLAUS
SANTA
DEDICATION
RESOURCEFUL
CHARITIES
ABUNDANCE
NORTH
POLE
WINTER
INNOVATION

"The North Pole collaboration between Mr. Grant Money and Santa Claus demonstrated the incredible potential of teamwork and innovative thinking. Their heartwarming adventure reminds us that with dedication and creativity, we can find enchanting solutions to our most challenging problems."

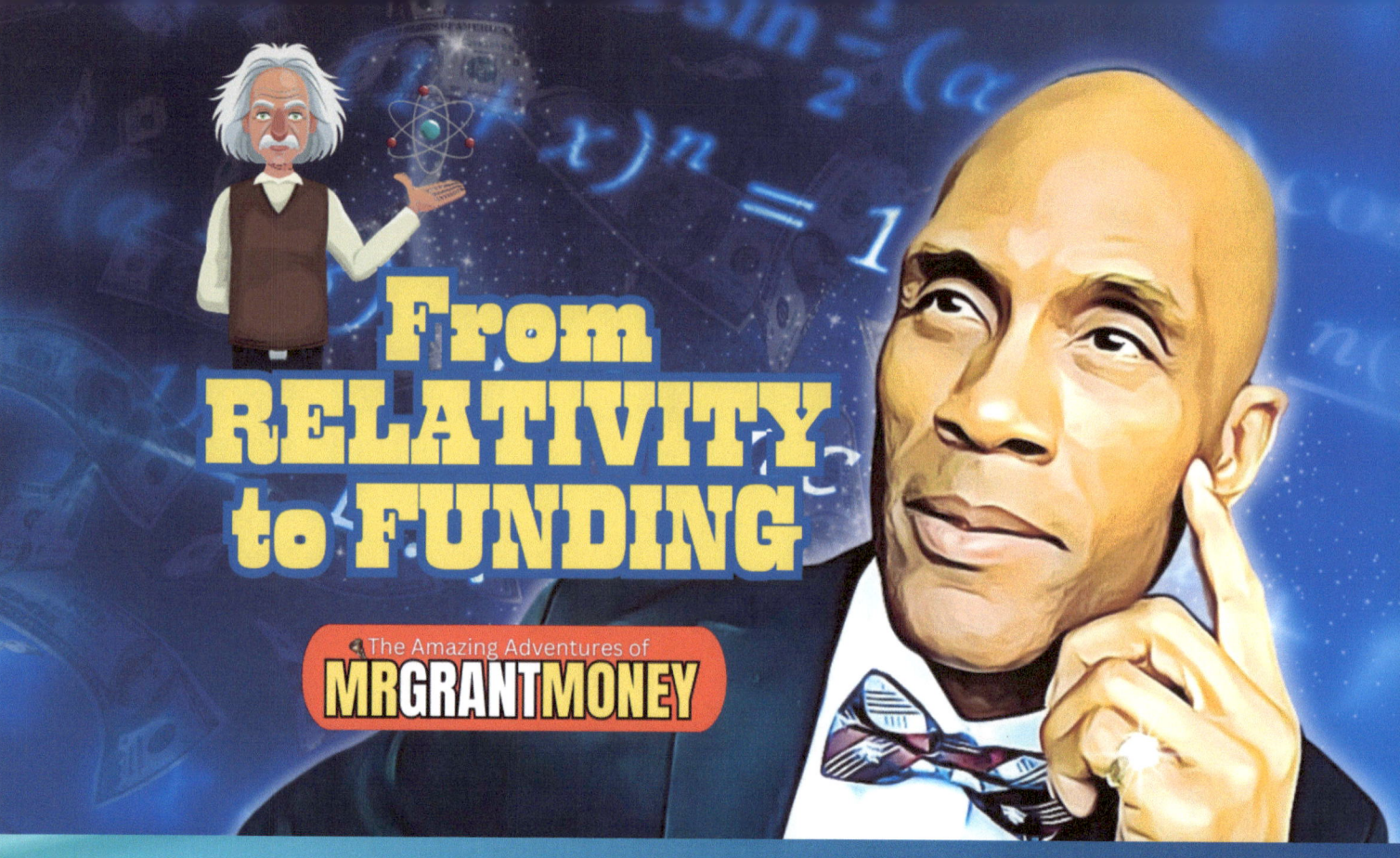

From Relativity to Funding: Mr. Grant Money's Journey

Unraveling the Mysteries of Funding with Einstein

After a whirlwind adventure through the glitz and glamour of Hollywood, Mr. Grant Money felt an inexplicable pull toward a different kind of star power. He found himself drawn to the hallowed halls of Cal Tech University, where a unique and electrifying energy seemed to crackle in the air. Little did he know that this journey would lead him to a remarkable encounter with one of the greatest minds in history.

As he stepped onto the campus, Mr. Grant Money was enveloped by an atmosphere of intellectual curiosity and innovation. The towering buildings seemed to hum with the echoes of groundbreaking discoveries. He strolled through the historic corridors, captivated by the sense of possibility that filled the air.

To his astonishment, he soon found himself standing in front of a classroom that bore a plaque commemorating the time when none other than Albert Einstein had taught there. It was as if the spirit of scientific exploration had guided him to this very spot. Intrigued and inspired, Mr. Grant Money decided to explore further.

His next stop was the former residence and office of Albert Einstein on Green Street. As he ascended the creaking wooden stairs to the second floor, he couldn't help but feel a sense of reverence. The walls of this historic place seemed to hold secrets and stories of a genius who had forever changed our understanding of the universe.

Mr. Grant Money finally arrived at Einstein's former office, adorned with a framed photograph of the physicist himself. Little did he know that what awaited him inside would be a conversation transcending time and space, filled with humor, wisdom, and the profound insights of a scientific icon.

As Mr. Grant Money stood in front of Albert Einstein's former office, he could feel the energy of the great physicist enveloping him. It was as if the very walls held the echoes of Einstein's groundbreaking thoughts. As he gazed at the photograph, a strange sensation washed over him. Suddenly, he found himself in a spirited conversation with none other than Einstein himself.

Einstein, with his unruly white hair and trademark mustache, looked at Mr. Grant Money with a twinkle in his eye. "Ah, my dear friend, it's not often I have the pleasure of conversing with someone from the world of grants."

Mr. Grant Money couldn't help but chuckle. "Likewise, Professor. Your contributions to science have had a profound impact on the world, much like the impact grants can have on communities."

Einstein nodded sagely. "Indeed, the law of relativity can be applied to many aspects of life, including grant acquisition. You see, everything is relative. What may seem impossible at first glance can be achieved with the right perspective and approach."

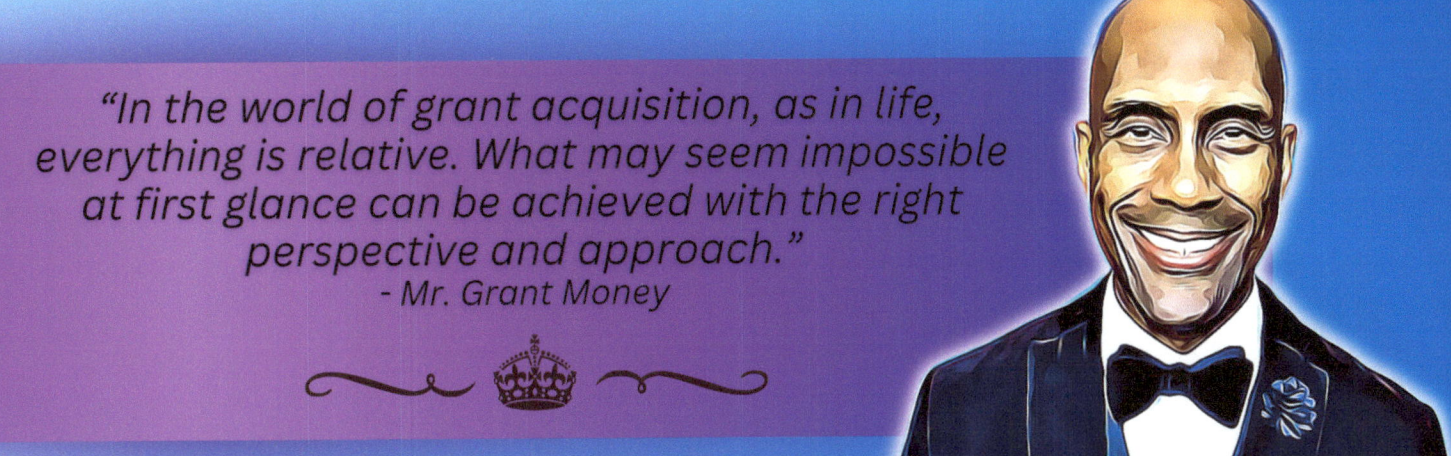

"In the world of grant acquisition, as in life, everything is relative. What may seem impossible at first glance can be achieved with the right perspective and approach."
- Mr. Grant Money

Mr. Grant Money leaned in, eager to soak up every word of wisdom from the renowned physicist. "So, Professor, what advice do you have for those seeking grants?" einstein's eyes sparkled with mischief. "Well, my dear friend, remember that creativity knows no bounds. Think beyond the conventional, and you may just uncover the solution you seek. And of course, persistence is key. Just as I pursued my theories relentlessly, so too must one persist in the pursuit of grants."

Mr. Grant Money nodded, absorbing every nugget of wisdom. "Thank you, Professor. Your insights are invaluable, and I will carry them with me on my journey."

As the conversation came to an end, Einstein smiled warmly. "It has been a pleasure, my friend. Remember, the key to success lies not only in knowledge, but in the boldness to apply it."

With a final exchange of gratitude, Mr. Grant Money found himself back in Einstein's former office, clutching his cherished scepter. The encounter had been surreal, but the lessons were very real indeed. As he left the historic house on Green Street, he couldn't help but feel a renewed sense of purpose and determination in his quest to secure grants for those in need.

"Remember, the key to success lies not only in knowledge but in the boldness to apply it." - A reflection on Einstein's wisdom."
- Mr. Grant Money

Exercise: "Einstein's Perspective - Relativity to Grant Acquisition"

This exercise is inspired by the wisdom shared by Albert Einstein and Mr. Grant Money during their extraordinary encounter. It encourages you to explore creative thinking, persistence, and applying a relative perspective to grant acquisition.

Objective: Embrace the wisdom of Einstein to enhance your grant acquisition efforts, think creatively, and maintain persistence.

Steps:

1. Creative Brainstorming Session:
- Gather a group of colleagues, friends, or peers who are involved in grant acquisition or share your interests in this area.

2. Relativity in Grant Acquisition:
- Begin the session by discussing the concept of relativity in the context of grant acquisition. Explore the idea that everything is relative, and what may seem impossible at first glance can be achieved with a different perspective.

3. Creative Problem-Solving:
- Encourage the group to identify a challenging grant acquisition problem or obstacle that your organization or group is currently facing.

4. Bold and Unconventional Idea:
- Following Einstein's advice, prompt participants to generate bold, creative, and unconventional solutions to the identified problem. Encourage them to think beyond the conventional and explore new approaches.

5. The Power of Persistence:
- Discuss the role of persistence in achieving goals. Share stories or examples of how persistence has led to successful grant acquisition in the past.

6. Incorporating Einstein's Wisdom:
- Encourage participants to incorporate the wisdom shared by Einstein during his encounter with Mr. Grant Money. How can creativity and persistence be applied to the grant acquisition challenges they face?

7. Interactive Activities:
- Engage in interactive activities or brainstorming sessions that promote creative thinking, such as mind mapping, role-playing, or brainstorming techniques like the "6 Thinking Hats" method.

8. Actionable Strategies:
- As a group, identify actionable strategies or solutions that have the potential to overcome the grant acquisition challenge you discussed at the beginning of the session.

9. Assignment and Follow-Up:
- Assign specific tasks or responsibilities to participants to implement the identified strategies or solutions. Set deadlines and follow up to track progress.

10. Reflection and Learning:
- Reconvene after a set period to reflect on the results of the implemented strategies. Discuss what worked well, what needs improvement, and any valuable lessons learned from the experience.

11. Documentation and Adaptation:
- Document the creative solutions, successful practices, and insights gained from this exercise. Adapt these lessons into your grant acquisition processes and practices.

By engaging in this exercise, you'll harness the wisdom of Einstein to approach grant acquisition challenges with creativity, persistence, and a relative perspective. This can lead to innovative solutions and more effective grant acquisition strategies, just as Einstein's revolutionary thinking transformed our understanding of the universe.

> "Remember, give your best each day and watch the compound effect of doing this one thing over time. You will become the best version of yourself."
> - Mr. Grant Money

Discussion Questions

1. Mr. Grant Money has a surreal encounter with Albert Einstein and learns valuable insights about applying the theory of relativity to grant acquisition. How do you interpret the idea that "everything is relative" in the context of grant-seeking and philanthropy? Can you provide examples from your own experiences where adopting a different perspective or thinking creatively led to grant success?

2. Albert Einstein emphasizes the importance of persistence and thinking beyond the conventional when seeking grants. How has persistence played a role in your grant acquisition efforts? Have you ever had to challenge conventional thinking or adopt an unconventional approach to secure funding for a project or initiative?

3. The story explores the idea that knowledge, while important, becomes truly valuable when applied boldly. How do you personally apply knowledge and insights gained from your experiences in grant acquisition? Can you share specific instances where applying knowledge led to positive outcomes in securing grants or philanthropic support?

4. Albert Einstein is known for his contributions to science and the theory of relativity. How can principles from the world of science and innovation be applied to the field of grant acquisition? Are there any parallels between scientific inquiry and the process of seeking funding for projects or charitable causes?

5. The story suggests that a visit to a historical place can inspire and provide valuable insights. Have you ever had a similar experience where a physical location or historical context influenced your approach to grant acquisition? How did that experience impact your strategies and outcomes in securing grants?

 Big Idea " The Quantum Leap Grant Challenge"

Create "The Quantum Leap Grant Challenge," a competitive initiative encouraging grant seekers to propose projects that represent a quantum leap in addressing social challenges. This challenge, inspired by the principles of quantum physics, seeks to elevate grant-funded projects that disrupt traditional models and bring about transformative change in unexpected ways.

🔍 Word Search

Embark on an intellectual journey with Mr. Grant Money as he visits the hallowed halls of Cal Tech University and has a remarkable encounter with the great physicist, Albert Einstein. In this word search puzzle, you'll discover 14 words inspired by their profound conversation and the spirit of scientific exploration.

In this puzzle, discover the words related to the extraordinary adventures of Mr. Grant Money. Can you find all the hidden words that capture the essence of this remarkable story?

Now, here are the 14 words for the word search puzzle based on the story:

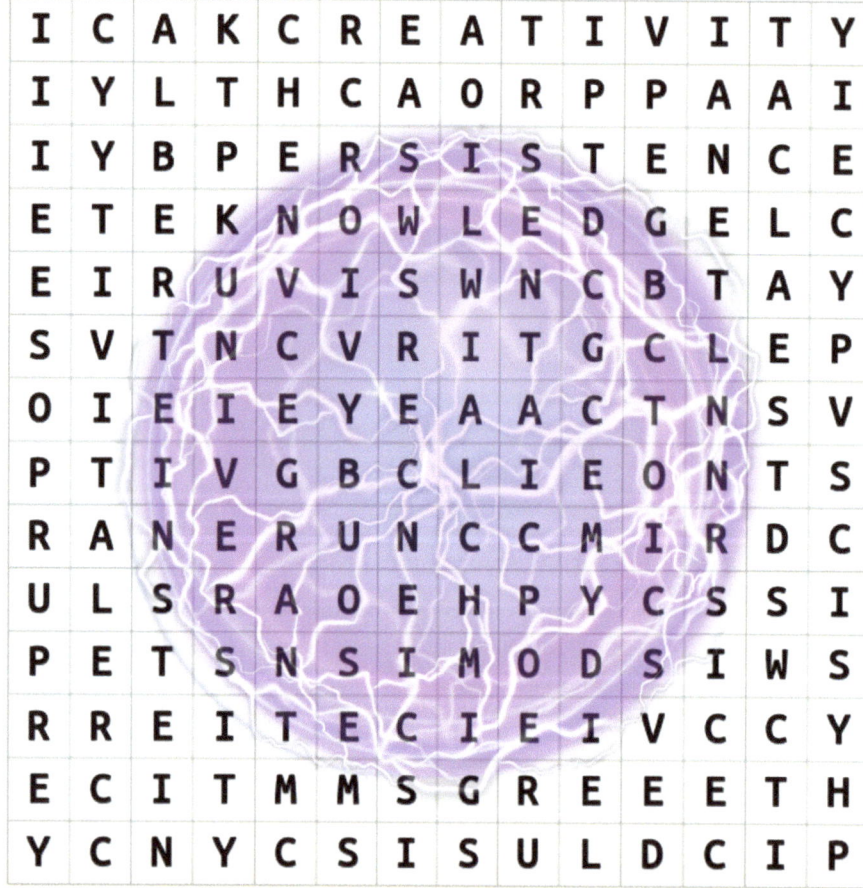

CAL TECH
KNOWLEDGE
APPROACH
ALBERTEINSTEIN
WISDOM
GRANT
UNIVERSITY
PERSISTENCE
SCIENCE
CREATIVITY
PURPOSE
PHYSICS
RELATIVITY
MONEY

"Persistence and determination backed by a solid game plan helps to win the prize. Go for the prize and enjoy the journey!"
—Mr. Grant Money

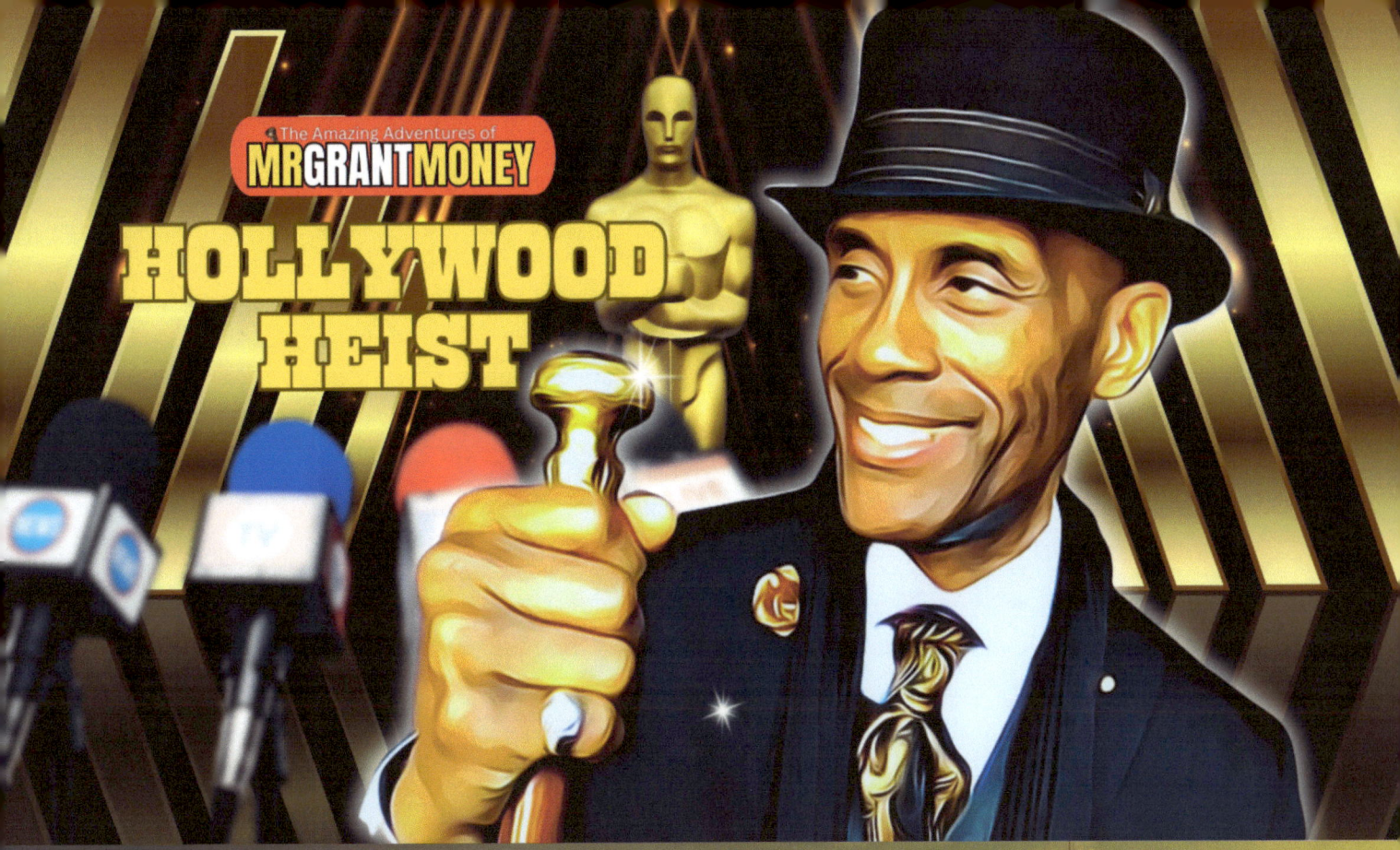

Mr. Grant Money's Hollywood Heist: The Golden Ticket Caper

Crashing the Emmy Awards Banquet with Style

The 64th Emmy Awards Show was a dazzling spectacle of glitz, glamour, and all things Hollywood. As the stars paraded down the red carpet, camera flashes illuminated the night, and Mr. Grant Money, true to his impeccably stylish self, graced the event like a seasoned celebrity.

Reporters and interviewers flocked to him, curious about this enigmatic figure who had effortlessly inserted himself into the heart of Hollywood's biggest night. Questions flew at him like rapid-fire rounds, and he fielded them with grace and charm.

"Mr. Grant Money, who are you wearing tonight?" asked a fashion correspondent.

"Why, it's a one-of-a-kind ensemble, darling, crafted by none other than Mr. GQ himself," he quipped with a wink.

As he continued to chat with various stars, they couldn't help but be drawn to his aura of mystique. They were charmed by his charisma, but eventually, the conversation turned to the banquet that followed the awards show.

"Mr. Grant Money, we'll be seated at Table 9 for the banquet. Where will you be?" inquired a renowned actress.

Mr. Grant Money, with a sly smile, realized he hadn't secured a ticket to the banquet. But he was never one to shy away from a challenge. In a quick, covert operation that would make James Bond proud, he deployed his creative and ingenious problem-solving skills.

He made a quick call on his stylish smartphone, and within moments, a discreet, well-dressed courier appeared by his side. In hushed tones, Mr. Grant Money instructed the courier to fetch his golden invitation to the banquet.

The courier nodded and swiftly vanished into the bustling crowd. Minutes later, he returned, discreetly slipping an envelope into Mr. Grant Money's hand. Inside was a golden ticket to the prestigious banquet, along with a handwritten note.

With his characteristic charm, Mr. Grant Money turned to the actress and said, "Darling, I believe I'll be joining you at Table 9, after all."

As the stars chuckled in amusement, Mr. Grant Money strolled into the banquet hall, a master of creativity and resourcefulness.

The lesson? In grant acquisition, just like in any endeavor, creativity and ingenuity often hold the key to solving complex problems. Sometimes, thinking outside the box and making strategic connections can secure the golden ticket to success, whether it's a Hollywood banquet or funding for a worthy cause.

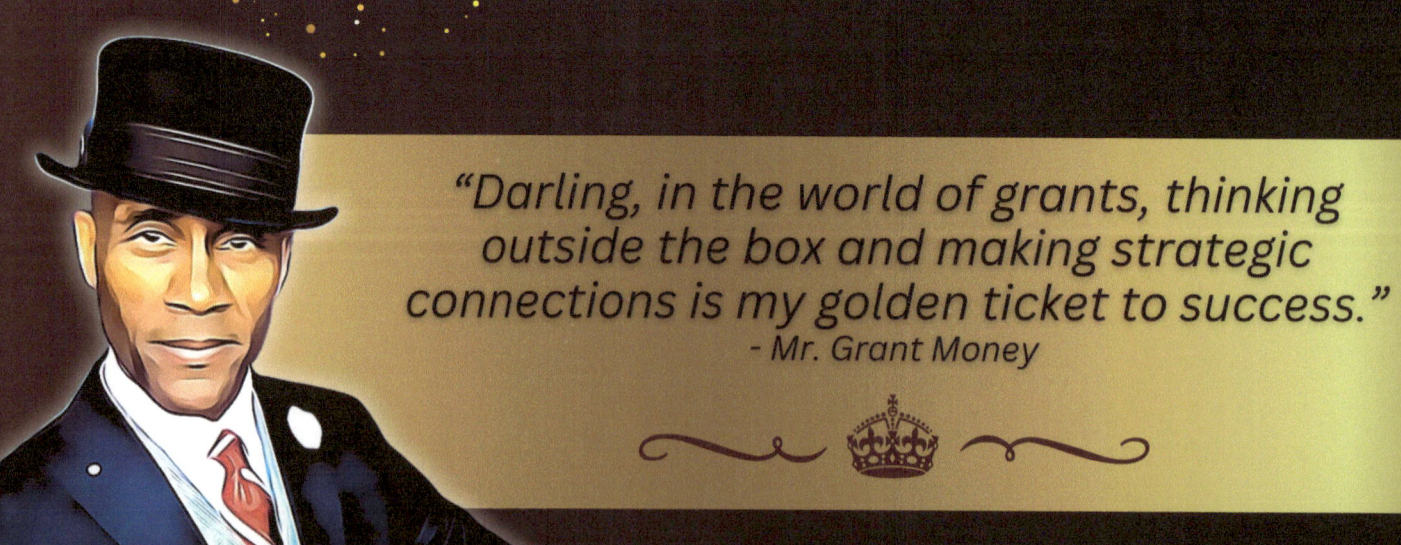

> "Darling, in the world of grants, thinking outside the box and making strategic connections is my golden ticket to success."
> - Mr. Grant Money

Exercise: "Securing the Golden Ticket: A Creative Problem-Solving Challenge"

This exercise draws inspiration from Mr. Grant Money's Hollywood heist and encourages participants to apply creative and ingenious problem-solving skills in the context of grant acquisition.

Objective: Develop participants' creative thinking and problem-solving abilities while highlighting the importance of thinking outside the box in grant acquisition.

Steps:

1. Set the Stage:
- Create a fun and engaging atmosphere reminiscent of a glamorous Hollywood event, with decorations and an awards show theme.

2. Introduction:
- Share the story of Mr. Grant Money's Hollywood heist and how his creativity and resourcefulness secured him a golden ticket to the banquet. Emphasize that creativity often holds the key to success, whether in Hollywood or grant acquisition.

3. The Challenge:
- Divide participants into small teams (or individuals, depending on the group size). Present them with a fictional but complex grant acquisition challenge that involves an unexpected obstacle or requirement. For example, securing a grant with a last-minute deadline, limited resources, or a unique condition.

4. Golden Ticket Hunt:
- Explain that their goal is to secure the "golden ticket" to overcome this grant acquisition challenge. The golden ticket could symbolize a solution or resource that they need to find.

5. Brainstorming and Planning:
- Give participants time to brainstorm and plan their approach to the challenge. Encourage them to think creatively and consider unconventional solutions.

6. Resource Exchange:
- Introduce a resource exchange component where participants can "trade" resources or information with other teams. This simulates the strategic connections Mr. Grant Money made with the courier in the story.

7. Solution Presentation:
- Each team or participant presents their solution to the challenge, explaining the creative strategies and resources they used to secure their "golden ticket."

8. Peer Evaluation:
- After each presentation, encourage participants to provide feedback and evaluate the creativity and effectiveness of their peers' solutions.

9. Discussion:
- Facilitate a group discussion on the lessons learned. Ask participants to reflect on how creativity and ingenious problem-solving can be applied to real-life grant acquisition challenges.

10. Application to Real Grant Challenges:
- Discuss with participants how the creative strategies they used in this exercise can be adapted to address actual grant acquisition challenges they may encounter in their work.

11. Action Plans:
- Have participants create action plans to implement the creative problem-solving techniques they learned in their grant acquisition projects.

12. Reflection:
- Conclude the exercise with a reflection session where participants share insights, personal takeaways, and the impact of creative thinking on grant acquisition.

By engaging in this exercise, participants will develop their creative problem-solving skills, learn to think outside the box, and apply innovative approaches to grant acquisition challenges. The "golden ticket" concept serves as a memorable and fun way to emphasize the value of creative thinking and resourcefulness in grant acquisition.

Discussion Questions

1. Mr. Grant Money's Hollywood heist at the Emmy Awards illustrates the importance of creative problem-solving and resourcefulness. Can you share an example from your own experiences where thinking outside the box and making strategic connections helped you overcome a challenge in grant acquisition or fundraising?

2. Mr. Grant Money used a discreet courier to fetch his golden invitation to the banquet. In the world of grant acquisition, effective networking and connections can be critical. How do you approach building and maintaining relationships with potential donors, grant organizations, or partners? What strategies have you found successful in securing the invitations (funding opportunities) you need?

3. The story highlights Mr. Grant Money's charisma and charm in handling unexpected situations. How do you believe personal qualities like charm, charisma, and adaptability impact one's effectiveness in grant acquisition or fundraising? What other personal attributes do you consider important in this field?

4. Mr. Grant Money's golden ticket to the banquet served as a metaphor for the concept that creativity and ingenuity can open doors to success. Can you provide an example where an innovative approach to grant acquisition or fundraising led to a significant accomplishment or opportunity? What strategies do you use to foster creativity and out-of-the-box thinking within your team or organization?

5. The story portrays Mr. Grant Money as a master of creativity and resourcefulness, who doesn't let obstacles deter him from achieving his goals. What advice would you give to individuals or teams engaged in grant acquisition or fundraising to cultivate a similar mindset of perseverance and adaptability? Can you share any personal experiences or challenges where perseverance was key to your success in this field?

💡 Big Idea "The Golden Ticket Grant Program"

Introduce "The Golden Ticket Grant Program," a funding initiative that symbolizes exclusive access to resources and opportunities. This program, inspired by Mr. Grant Money's acquisition of a golden ticket to the banquet, would offer a select number of grants with additional support and visibility, elevating chosen projects to greater success.

🔍 Word Search

Step into the glitzy world of Hollywood and the 64th Emmy Awards Show, where Mr. Grant Money showcased his impeccable style and resourcefulness. As you embark on this word search puzzle, you'll uncover 15 words that capture the essence of Hollywood glamour, creativity, and clever problem-solving.

In this puzzle, discover the words related to the extraordinary adventures of Mr. Grant Money. Can you find all the hidden words that capture the essence of this remarkable story?

Now, here are the 15 words for the word search puzzle based on the story:

T	U	L	T	N	A	R	G	T	K	E	Z	L	D
C	E	M	H	O	L	L	Y	W	O	O	D	T	E
R	C	H	A	L	L	E	N	G	E	G	E	R	L
E	E	G	L	A	M	O	U	R	R	R	L	L	S
I	E	E	H	S	U	E	Z	Y	Y	H	V	R	E
S	C	E	L	E	B	R	I	T	Y	M	L	S	A
T	L	U	F	E	C	R	U	O	S	E	R	M	R
Y	H	W	C	H	A	R	I	S	M	A	Z	O	N
L	T	E	P	R	A	C	D	E	R	S	S	E	L
I	S	U	C	C	E	S	S	A	S	D	D	G	G
S	L	S	E	U	Q	I	T	S	Y	M	C	L	L
H	C	R	E	A	T	I	V	E	A	U	I	R	G
M	O	T	L	T	I	C	K	E	T	T	H	A	C
Y	E	N	O	M	E	O	I	O	Z	Y	T	C	U

CELEBRITY
RED CARPET
GRANT
STYLISH
MYSTIQUE
GLITZ
CHALLENGE
TICKET
GLAMOUR
CHARISMA
RESOURCEFUL
CREATIVE
SUCCESS
HOLLYWOOD
MONEY

"In the world of high-stakes events, sometimes, thinking creatively and making strategic connections can be the golden ticket to unlocking new possibilities."

Mr. Grant Money's Aussie Adventure: Outback Triumph

Tackling Conservation Challenges in the Australian Wilderness

Down Under, in the heart of Australia, Mr. Grant Money embarked on an adventure that was both funny and exhilarating. He had been summoned to assist a consortium of environmental nonprofits striving to secure funding for their ambitious conservation project in the rugged Outback.

As he touched down in Sydney, Mr. Grant Money couldn't help but marvel at the stunning Sydney Opera House and the iconic Sydney Harbour Bridge. However, there was no time for sightseeing just yet; the Outback beckoned.

The journey into the wilderness was nothing short of an epic Australian safari. With his stylish attire adjusted for the dusty trails and harsh sun, Mr. Grant Money joined the conservationists in their mission to protect the unique wildlife and pristine landscapes of the Outback.

Their quest took them deep into the heart of the wilderness, where they encountered kangaroos hopping gracefully across the vast plains, koalas clinging to eucalyptus trees, and colorful parrots soaring overhead. But amidst the beauty of the Outback, they faced their share of challenges.

One day, while attempting to navigate a particularly treacherous river crossing, their four-wheel-drive vehicle became stuck in the mud. With the vehicle wheels spinning fruitlessly, and the scorching Australian sun beating down, the situation was starting to look dire.

However, Mr. Grant Money, always the resourceful problem-solver, had a trick up his impeccably tailored sleeve. He reached into his trusty leather briefcase and pulled out a compact but powerful winch. Attaching it to a sturdy tree, he expertly maneuvered the winch, and with a mighty heave, the vehicle was freed from the mud, much to the relief of the team.

Their adventure continued, and as they camped under the star-studded Australian night sky, Mr. Grant Money shared valuable insights with the conservationists. He emphasized the importance of resilience and adaptability in the face of unforeseen challenges, much like the Australian wildlife they were striving to protect.

Back in Sydney, with funding secured for the conservation project, Mr. Grant Money bid farewell to the Outback. He couldn't help but smile as he looked back at the funny and adventurous journey he had undertaken.

The teachable moment? Grant acquisition, like navigating the Australian wilderness, often requires adaptability, resilience, and the ability to overcome unexpected obstacles. Just as Mr. Grant Money had his trusty winch, grant seekers should be prepared with the right tools, strategies, and a sense of adventure to tackle the challenges that come their way.

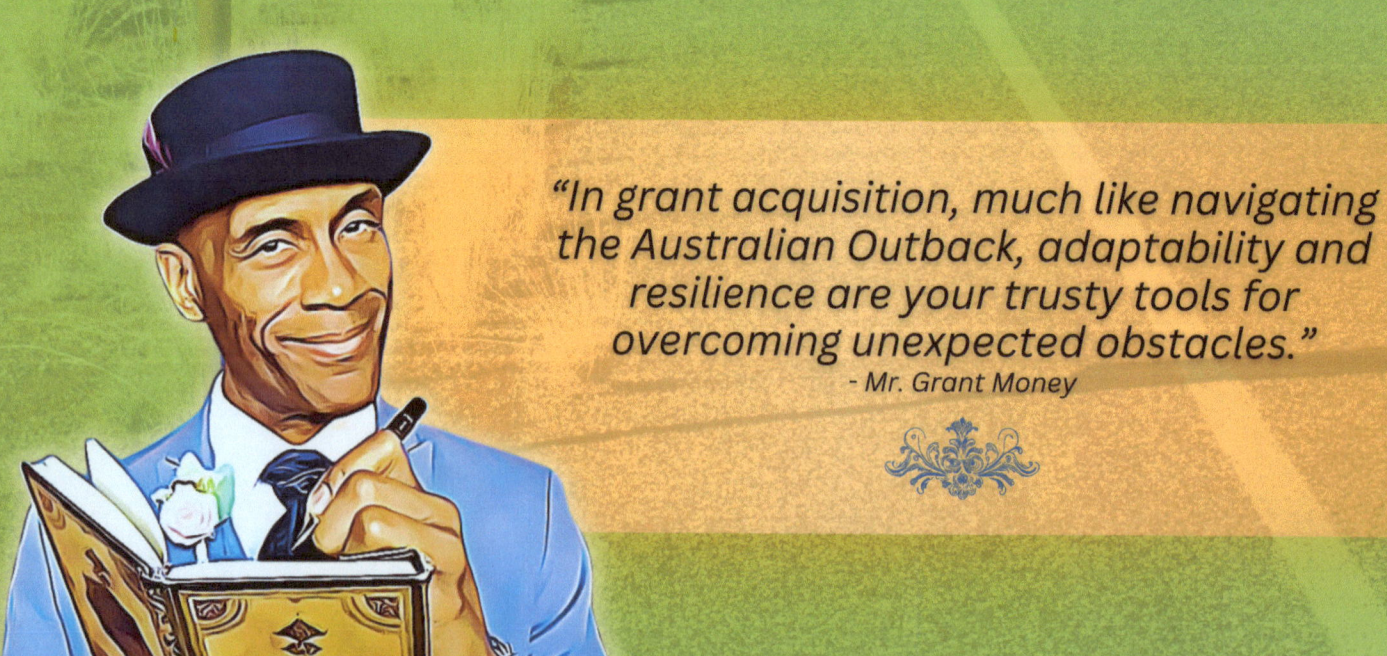

"In grant acquisition, much like navigating the Australian Outback, adaptability and resilience are your trusty tools for overcoming unexpected obstacles."
- Mr. Grant Money

Exercise: "Adaptability and Resilience Challenge"

This exercise draws inspiration from Mr. Grant Money's adventure in the Australian Outback and encourages participants to develop adaptability and resilience in the context of grant acquisition.

Objective: Develop participants' abilities to adapt to unforeseen challenges and demonstrate resilience when facing obstacles during grant acquisition.

Steps:

1. Introduce the Challenge:
- Share the story of Mr. Grant Money's adventure in the Australian Outback and the challenges he faced. Emphasize the importance of adaptability and resilience.

2. Scenario Setting:
- Present participants with a fictional grant acquisition scenario that involves an unexpected obstacle. This could be a sudden change in grant requirements, a missed deadline, or an unforeseen budget constraint.

3. Adaptation Brainstorm:
- Divide participants into small teams. Each team's task is to brainstorm and plan how they would adapt to the challenge presented in the scenario. Encourage creative thinking and resourcefulness.

4. Obstacle Cards:
- Prepare a set of "obstacle cards" with various challenges related to grant acquisition. Each team draws one card, and the challenge on the card becomes the obstacle they must address in their scenario.

5. Resource Allocation:
- Assign each team a set of limited resources (e.g., time, budget, personnel) to simulate real-world constraints. Teams must factor in these resources while developing their adaptation plans.

6. Solution Presentation:
- Each team presents its adaptation plan for overcoming the obstacle, explaining their strategies and the resource allocation choices they made.

7. Peer Evaluation:
- After each presentation, encourage participants to provide feedback and evaluate the creativity and effectiveness of their peers' adaptation plans.

8. Discussion:
- Facilitate a group discussion on the lessons learned. Ask participants to share their insights into the challenges they encountered and how they applied adaptability and resilience in their solutions.

9. Action Plans:
- Have participants create action plans to implement the adaptability and resilience strategies they practiced in their future grant acquisition projects.

10. Reflection:
- Conclude the exercise with a reflection session where participants share personal takeaways, key learnings, and the importance of adaptability and resilience in grant acquisition.

By engaging in this exercise, participants will develop their problem-solving skills, adaptability, and resilience, which are vital qualities for addressing unexpected challenges in grant acquisition. The use of obstacle cards and limited resources adds a dynamic and engaging component to the exercise, helping participants simulate real-world situations in a fun and interactive manner.

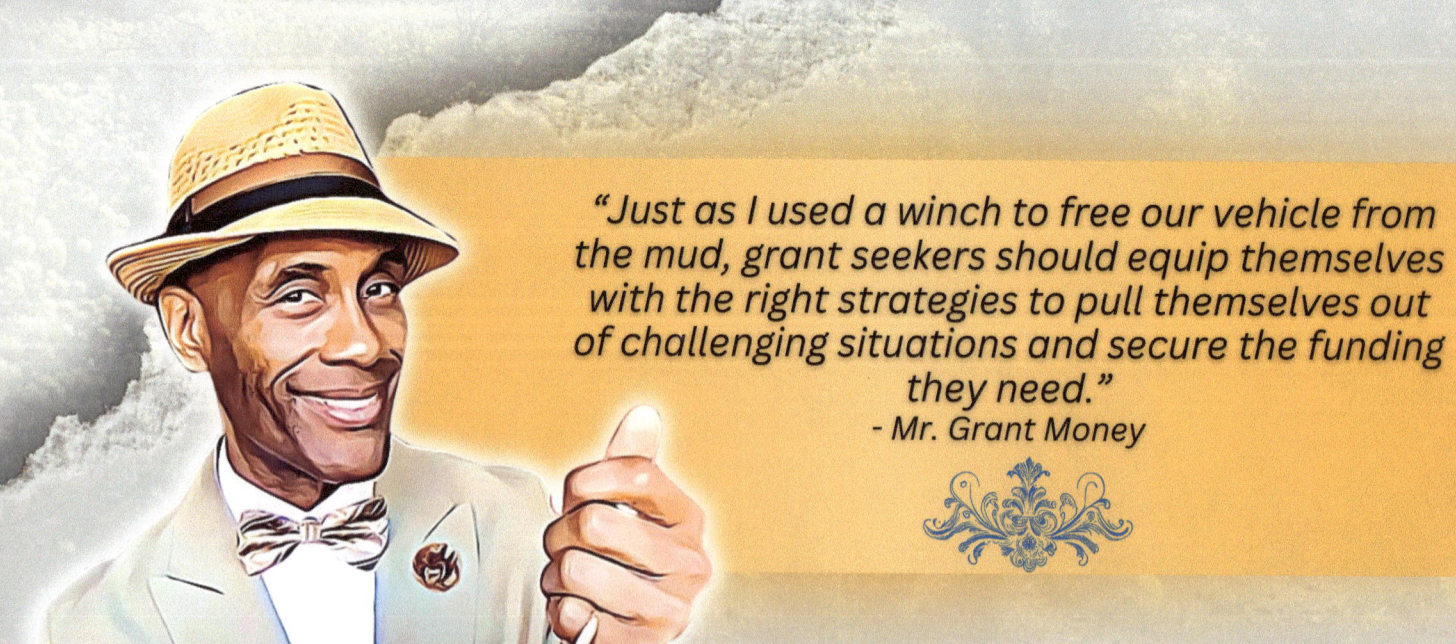

"Just as I used a winch to free our vehicle from the mud, grant seekers should equip themselves with the right strategies to pull themselves out of challenging situations and secure the funding they need."
- Mr. Grant Money

Discussion Questions

1. Mr. Grant Money's Australian adventure emphasized the importance of adaptability and resilience when facing unforeseen challenges. Can you share a personal experience in the world of grant acquisition or fundraising where your ability to adapt to unexpected obstacles was crucial in achieving your goals?

2. The story showcases Mr. Grant Money's resourcefulness in using a winch to overcome a challenging situation in the Outback. In grant acquisition, what tools, strategies, or resources do you find most valuable in overcoming obstacles or setbacks? How important is it to have a plan in place to address unexpected challenges in the grant-seeking process?

3. While camping under the star-studded Australian night sky, Mr. Grant Money shared insights with the conservationists. What do you consider the most important lessons or principles in grant acquisition or fundraising that you've learned throughout your experiences? How have these lessons helped you achieve success in your field?

4. The story highlights the conservationists' mission to protect the unique wildlife and landscapes of the Australian Outback. Can you discuss the significance of conservation initiatives and their relationship to grant acquisition or fundraising? How does raising funds for such causes impact communities, ecosystems, or society as a whole?

5. In the end, Mr. Grant Money's adventure reinforces the idea that grant acquisition often requires adaptability, resilience, and the right tools or strategies. What advice would you give to individuals or organizations engaged in grant-seeking to foster these qualities and be better prepared for unexpected challenges or opportunities? Can you share any specific strategies or approaches that have worked well for you in this context?

 Big Idea "The AI-Powered Grant Proposal Analyzer"

Introduce an "AI-Powered Grant Proposal Analyzer" that uses natural language processing and machine learning to evaluate and optimize grant proposals. This tool would provide instant feedback, identify potential weaknesses, and suggest improvements, ultimately increasing the likelihood of a successful grant application.

🔍 Word Search

Prepare to venture into the heart of Australia's rugged Outback alongside Mr. Grant Money. His humorous and exhilarating journey through this stunning wilderness serves as the backdrop for a word search puzzle that encapsulates the spirit of resilience and adaptability. Discover 15 words that mirror the challenges and excitement of this adventure.

In this puzzle, discover the words related to the extraordinary adventures of Mr. Grant Money. Can you find all the hidden words that capture the essence of this remarkable story?

Now, here are the 15 words for the word search puzzle based on the story:

```
C C O N S E R V A T I O N R
H F A D A P T A B I L I T Y
A A A E L G I W P E C E L E
L D T T A L K I N V Y O R N
L V O O I A A L A O K A H U
E E A R T I O D H B A W N O
N N A R D L U E A F I I P K
G T M A S A T R H U R H I A
E U O P A R B N H N A C R N
T R N B N T A E O D N N T G
N E E Y O S C S M I I I O A
A N Y C N U K S N N N W O R
R K E O N A W E R G I A G O
G A R E S I L I E N C E V O
```

ADAPTABILITY
FUNDING
RESILIENCE
WILDERNESS
CHALLENGE
CONSERVATION
ADVENTURE
PARROT
KOALA
MONEY
KANGAROO
OUTBACK
AUSTRALIA
GRANT
WINCH

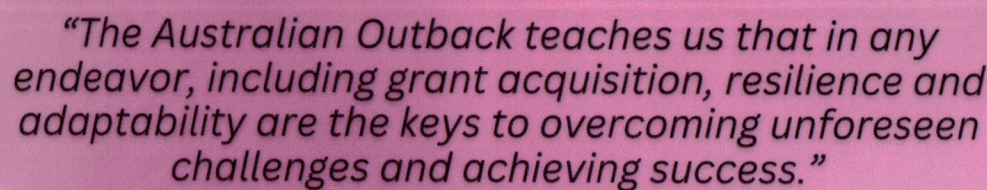

"The Australian Outback teaches us that in any endeavor, including grant acquisition, resilience and adaptability are the keys to overcoming unforeseen challenges and achieving success."

AFTERWARD

Congratulations, on completing yet another exhilarating volume of Mr. Grant Money's adventures, "Grant Odyssey." As you reflect on the remarkable stories within, you've journeyed through time and space, expanding your understanding of grant acquisition in ways you never thought possible.

In this volume, Mr. Grant Money's time-traveling feats have showcased the immense power of history in shaping our present and future. The past is a treasure trove of knowledge and inspiration, and as you've seen, it's a well that never runs dry. You're no longer bound to seeking solutions solely from the present; you can now tap into the vast history that surrounds you, drawing wisdom from the ages.

The stories you've encountered are not just tales of whimsy. They are lessons, painted with the brush of time and experience, which offer insight into grant acquisition, philanthropy, and life itself. The exercises, discussion questions, powerful quotes, and BIG Ideas have armed you with the tools to navigate the ever-changing landscape of grant writing with confidence and creativity.

The adventures of Mr. Grant Money have always been aimed at a diverse audience. Whether you're a seasoned grant professional, an aspiring grant writer, a consultant, a nonprofit organization representative, or anyone in between, you've found valuable lessons within these pages. These lessons are adaptable, capable of fitting seamlessly into your unique grant acquisition journey.

Remember that "Grant Odyssey" is not a book that provides the mere technicalities of grant writing. It's an exploration into the human spirit and the depths of creativity, where past and present meld into the future. It is an invitation to be resourceful, resilient, and ready to tackle the challenges of grant acquisition with grace and style.

As you stand at the end of this volume, don't think of it as an ending, but as a new beginning. Your journey is far from over, and Volume 5 awaits your arrival. Your next set of adventures with Mr. Grant Money promises to be as exhilarating, enlightening, and engaging as those you've experienced so far.

Embrace the challenge, embark on new quests, and always remember that the vast tapestry of history is a tapestry of solutions. The answers you seek are not just in the present but are woven throughout the ages.

Consider the words of philosopher Seneca: "To the person who does not know where he wants to go, there is no favorable wind." Armed with the knowledge, experience, and wisdom gained from Mr. Grant Money's adventures, you know where you're headed. The favorable winds are at your back.

So, take a deep breath, step into the unknown, and keep seeking knowledge, embracing creativity, and striving for excellence in your grant acquisition journey. Your adventures, much like Mr. Grant Money's, have the potential to be extraordinary.

Onward to Volume 5, where new adventures and insights await.

ABOUT THE AUTHOR

Rodney Walker is a man on a mission. He's dedicated his life to helping others secure funding for their projects and dreams. As the President of Grant Central USA, a grant development training firm internationally known for helping organizations land six-figure and seven-figure grants and shave months off the time it takes to get funded, Rodney has helped clients raise over half a billion dollars in grants!

He's also an author of numerous books, online courses and the founder of two popular grant writing conferences: The Education Grants Conference and First Responders Grants Conference. Grant Central USA has also partnered with several universities, including Regis University, Hawaii University, Oklahoma University, National University, Cal Poly University, and Florida Atlantic University.

Rodney is even the host of four podcasts: Get Funded with Rodney, Grant Writing Today, Grant Business Show, and Schools Winning Grants. He oversees Grant Success Advisors, an elite network of approved licensees who deliver today's leading training in grant development systems.

He has an extensive network of high-level contacts, including his Grant Writers Association group on Linkedin with over 15,000+ members.

Considered a national authority in the grant industry, Grant Central USA's clients have included, The Magic Johnson Foundation, the George W. Bush Foundation, Ben Guillory and Danny Glover of the Robey Theatre Company, Hawaii State Teachers Association, United Way, Habitat for Humanity, and numerous school districts and city governments.

Rodney has produced over 730 videos on grant development on his popular YouTube channel and has taught over 240,000 people how to improve their grant writing efforts. "We have been helping our clients successfully get funded and launch new careers in grant writing since 2006 across the U.S. and worldwide, giving them both the competence and the confidence to win the grants at a high level."

He says his primary specialty is "Getting our clients funded with six-figure and seven-figure grants while helping grant professionals get paid what they are worth!"

In addition to his leadership experience at Grant Central USA, he has years of experience in Business and Professional Development in various sectors. He has been a sought-after expert in grant professional development, coaching, and the law of success.

As a media personality, he has interviewed numerous celebrities, including Snoop Dogg, Heisman Trophy Winners: Reggie Bush, Charles Woodson, Professional Boxer Laila Ali, America's Next Top Model Season 19 Winner: Laura James, NBA Champions: Draymond Green, Matt Barnes, National College Football Champions: Coach Mack Brown, and Vince Young, and countless others.

It's safe to say that Rodney knows his stuff regarding grants and working with champions!

GRANT MONEY MAGNET™

I am the Grant Money Magnet™, a relentless force that navigates the intricate maze of grant acquisition with unwavering determination and a strategic mind. Challenges are not obstacles; they are opportunities waiting to be seized. With every hurdle, I rise, armed with innovative solutions, pushing the boundaries of what's possible. My curiosity is my compass, guiding me through the maze of grant landscapes, uncovering hidden opportunities and transforming challenges into triumphs.

In the realm of grant development campaigns, I am the orchestrator of a symphony that goes beyond the basics of mere grant writing. My daily actions are a testament to my commitment, with well-defined grant goals propelling me forward. I am not a lone warrior; I am part of a powerful grant team, where collaboration amplifies our impact. Together, we transcend the ordinary, transforming aspirations into tangible results.

Grant funding doesn't elude me; I attract it with an irresistible magnetic force. My mind is a powerhouse of ideas, a generator of solutions that resonate with the aspirations of benefactors and the needs of society. Relentlessness is my mantra; there's no door I can't open, no avenue left unexplored. I don't just pursue grants; I nurture relationships, cultivating a network of allies who share my passion for impact. In my grant pursuit, I don't just raise funds; I raise friends and partners, forging alliances that extend beyond transactions into enduring collaborations.

As the architect of my grant destiny, I recognize that true power lies not just in acquiring funds but in the collective strength of a united effort. I am not merely a seeker of grants; I am a catalyst for transformative change. With each campaign, I etch my mark on the maze of philanthropy, weaving a narrative of impact that transcends the ordinary. Together with my grant team, I shape a future where challenges bow before innovation, and the resonance of our collaborative endeavors echoes through the corridors of progress. Grant by grant, we sculpt a legacy that stands as a testament to the limitless potential of unified action and unwavering dedication.

Recite and embrace the power of this statement daily; let its resonance shape your mindset and fuel your unwavering commitment to grant success.

GRANTOPOLY ROYAL RULES

Dive into a realm of funding mastery with Mr. Grant Money's 10 Grantopoly Royal Rules For Engagement - your strategic guide to securing maximum funding for your organization. Revisit these rules often and witness your grant success soar as you put them into practice! 🚀 💰 #GrantMastery #FundingSuccess

1. 🎯 **Master the Mission:** Clearly articulate your organization's mission in every proposal, demonstrating an unwavering commitment to your cause.

2. 🌟 **Impact is King:** Highlight the tangible, life-changing impact of your projects; grantors want to see real results.

3. 🤝 **Build Strategic Alliances:** Showcase partnerships with other organizations to demonstrate a united front in achieving common goals.

4. 📊 **Data Speaks Louder:** Back your proposals with compelling data and statistics that underscore the urgency and necessity of your work.

5. 📖 **Storytelling Magic:** Craft narratives that evoke empathy, connecting the funder emotionally to your mission and beneficiaries.

6. 💰 **Budget Brilliance:** Develop meticulously detailed budgets that align with project goals and ensure every dollar is well-spent.

7. 📈 **Transparent Metrics:** Articulate clear and measurable outcomes, outlining how the funding will drive positive change.

8. 🌐 **Engage the Community:** Illustrate strong community involvement and support, reflecting a broad network invested in your success.

9. 🔄 **Continuous Learning:** Demonstrate a commitment to improvement through feedback loops and adaptive strategies.

10. 🙏 **Express Gratitude:** Always express sincere gratitude for the grantor's consideration, building a foundation for long-term partnerships.

MR. GRANT MONEY'S IDIOMS

Welcome to a world of financial creativity and linguistic flair! In this collection, you'll find ten unique "Mr. Grant Money" idioms crafted to add a touch of wit and imagination to your discussions about grants and funding opportunities. These idioms are not just expressions; they're windows into the dynamic and often challenging realm of grant acquisition. Enjoy more of these with new ones in the next volumes.

1. **Granting a Feather in One's Cap:**
Meaning: Achieving recognition or success in securing a particularly prestigious or competitive grant.

2. **The Grant Puzzle Palace:**
Meaning: Navigating the complex and interconnected aspects of grant applications and approvals.

3. **Whistling Past the Grant Graveyard:**
Meaning: Ignoring potential risks or challenges associated with grant projects.

4. **Granting the Golden Ticket:**
Meaning: Securing a highly coveted grant opportunity that opens doors to significant resources.

5. **Hitting the Grant Jackpot:**
Meaning: Experiencing unexpected and substantial success in obtaining multiple grants.

6. **The Grant Alchemist:**
Meaning: Transforming modest grant funds into significant and lasting positive impacts.

7. **Granting the Symphony of Solutions:**
Meaning: Collaboratively addressing complex issues through a combination of grants and innovative solutions.

8. **Whispering Grants in the Moonlight:**
Meaning: Discussing or exploring potential grant opportunities in a secretive or discreet manner.

9. **Navigating Grant Rapids:**
Meaning: Maneuvering through rapidly changing conditions and requirements in the grant landscape.

10. **The Grant Phoenix Rises Again:**
Meaning: Overcoming setbacks and challenges to achieve success in securing grant funding.

INFORMATIONAL INTERVIEW

Informational interviews are an excellent way to gain valuable insights and knowledge from experienced grant professionals and grant makers. By engaging in conversations with experts in the field, you can enhance your understanding, learn best practices, and foster your continuous growth and development in the world of grant funding.

Instructions:

1. **Identify Potential Interviewees:**
   - Create a list of grant professionals, grant makers, and other individuals with relevant insights whom you would like to interview. Consider factors such as expertise, experience, and industry focus.

2. **Reach Out:**
   - Craft a polite and concise email introducing yourself and explaining your interest in an informational interview. Request a convenient time for a meeting, either in person, over the phone, or via video call.

3. **Prepare Questions:**
   - Develop a list of thoughtful questions to guide your conversation. Tailor these questions to the individual's expertise and experiences. Be sure to ask about challenges they've faced, successes they've had, and advice they can offer.

4. **Schedule the Interview:**
   - Once you receive a positive response, schedule a time for the informational interview. Be respectful of their time and come prepared with your questions.

5. **Conduct the Interview:**
   - During the interview, actively listen, take notes, and ask follow-up questions. Be respectful of their time constraints and focus on extracting valuable insights.

6. **Reflect and Analyze:**
   - After each interview, take some time to reflect on the key takeaways. Consider how the information can be applied to your own work and goals.

7. **Thank You Note:**
   - Send a thank-you email expressing your gratitude for their time and insights. Mention specific points from the interview that were particularly helpful.

INFORMATIONAL INTERVIEW

Interviewee Information:

Name:
Title:
Organization:
Contact Information:
Date of Interview:

Interview Questions:

1. What led you to pursue a career in grant writing /management/grant making?
2. Can you share a significant challenge you faced in your career and how you overcame it?
3. What are the key skills and qualities you believe are crucial for success in this field?
4. How do you stay updated on the latest trends and changes in the grant industry?
5. Can you provide insights into your most successful grant project? What made it successful?
6. What advice do you have for someone looking to advance their career in grant management/grant making?
7. Are there any common misconceptions about working in grant-related roles that you'd like to address?

Key Takeaways:

Learnings:
Actionable Steps:
Connections Made:

Next Steps:

Identify Additional Contacts:
Schedule Next Informational Interview:
Implement Insights into Your Work:

This worksheet is designed to guide you through the process of conducting informational interviews and extracting valuable information to support your continuous growth and development in the field of grant funding. Good luck!

Take Your Grant Game To The Next Level With These...

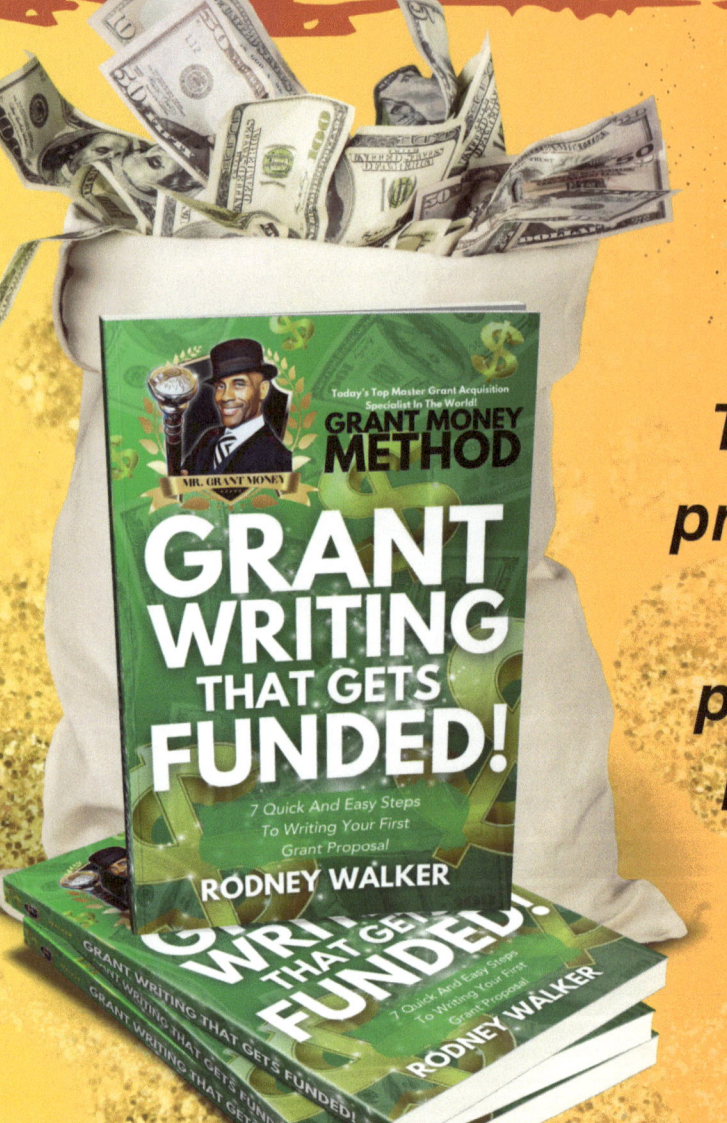

"Rodney is a grant genius! His courses are well thought out and clear, making the process of learning grant writing easier."
- Elena Esparza, Procurement/Contract Administrator

Transform your grant proposals into lucrative successes with my proven strategies that have raised millions.

"I hit my benchmark goal of $350,000.00!"
- Rebecca Laharia

"Thank you so much for your help. Probably not a day has gone by that I didn't use something."
- Evelyn Barker, Director of Grants and Special Project at University of Texas

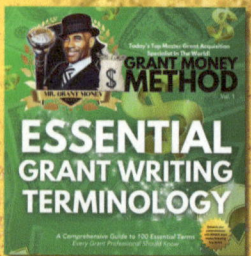   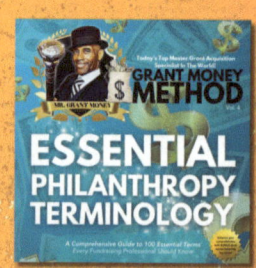 

Boost your confidence in grant writing, fundraising, and finance! Elevate your communication skills with the **Fundraising Fundamentals Vocabulary Builder Series** – *100 essential terms in each series.* Invest in knowledge, empower your success!

MGM Music to Get You Going 🎷 and 🎶 Keep You Soaring!

Music has the power to make life and learning more joyful. Get ready to have a blast with Mr. Grant Money Music, where every tune is fun, upbeat, and filled with positivity. These story-driven songs not only entertain but also educate and inspire, making your journey both enjoyable and enriching. 🎶

Dive into a symphony of stories and inspiration with Mr. Grant Money Music, where every note is a step toward greater success.

You can enjoy Mr. Grant Money Music on most major streaming platforms, including Spotify, Apple Music, and Amazon Music, bringing inspiration and positivity right to your favorite device. 🎧

Diverse Musical Flavors to Satisfy Every Listening Craving

Topical and Seasonal Themes
Enjoy our themed musical sessions that align with the seasons and current events, offering fresh perspectives and innovative ideas from today's Top Master Grant Acquisition Specialist, Mr. Grant Money!

Experience Our Other Dynamic Series with Mr. Grant Money!

Scholarship Odyssey: Mr. Grant Money's Roadmap
Vol. 1
ISBN 979-8-89725-000-4

Journey To Acceptance: Navigating College Applications
Vol. 2
ISBN 979-8-89725-001-1

Passion Into Practice: Specialized Scholarship
Vol. 3
ISBN 979-8-89725-002-8

Passport To Success: Navigating Global Scholarships
Vol. 4
ISBN 979-8-89725-003-5

Empowering Futures: Scholarships With Lasting Impact
Vol. 5
ISBN 979-8-89725-004-2

The Entrepreneurial Classroom: Teens Redefining Success
Vol. 1
ISBN 979-8-89725-005-9

Mindset Mastery: Developing The Teen Entrepreneurial Spirit
Vol. 2
ISBN 979-8-89725-006-6

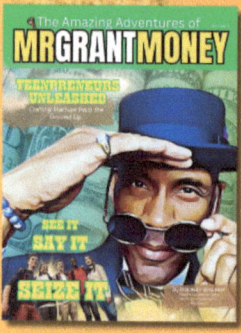
Teenpreneurs Unleashed: Crafting Startups From The Ground Up
Vol. 3
ISBN 979-8-89725-007-3

Business Battlefront: Teens Conquering Challenges In Startups
Vol. 4
ISBN 979-8-89725-008-0

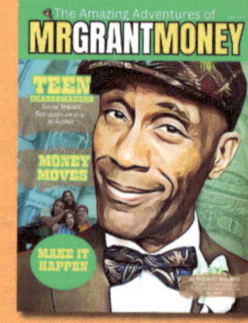
Teen Changemakers: Social Impact Entrepreneurship in Action
Vol. 5
ISBN 979-8-89725-009-7

Pocket Power: A Guide to Practical Budgeting for Teens
Vol. 1
ISBN 979-8-89725-010-3

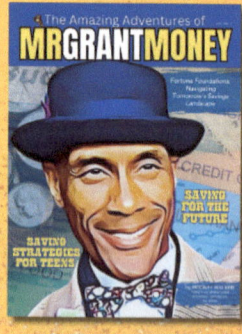
Fortune Foundations: Navigating Tomorrow's Savings Landscape
Vol. 2
ISBN 979-8-89725-011-0

Profit Pioneers: Young Entrepreneurs Unleashed
Vol. 3
ISBN 979-8-89725-012-7

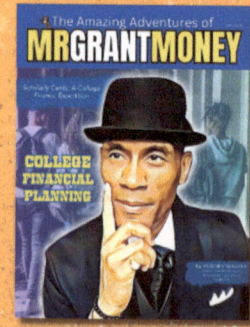
Scholarly Cents: A College Finance Expedition
Vol. 4
ISBN 979-8-89725-013-4

Financial Fortitude: Navigating Life's Financial Storm
Vol. 5
ISBN 979-8-89725-014-1

Enjoy More Amazing Adventures with Mr. Grant Money!

Harvesting Hope: The Global Odyssey of Mr. Grant Money
Vol. 1
ISBN 978-0-9659275-0-5

The Artful Navigator: Mr. Grant Money's Chronicles
Vol. 2
ISBN 978-0-9659275-2-9

Grantopoly: Mr. Grant Money's Out-of-This-World Wisdom
Vol. 3
ISBN 978-0-9659275-3-6

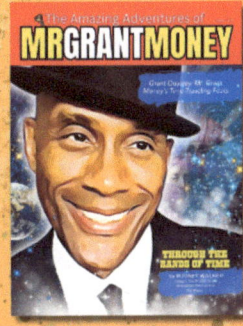
Grant Odyssey: Mr. Grant Money's Time-Traveling Feats
Vol. 4
ISBN 978-0-9659275-4-3

Unlocking Powerful Secrets of Grant Acquisition
Vol. 5
ISBN 978-0-9659275-5-0

Gain Exclusive Access To Companion Resources & Bonus Materials at MrGrantMoney.com and GrantCentralUsa.com

Bring the transformative Adventures and lessons of Mr. Grant Money to your educational institution or organization by **acquiring your license today**. Enjoy exclusive access to a wealth of online resources, such as special reports, worksheets, videos, audio training, discounts, and more, elevating the entire experience to the next level!

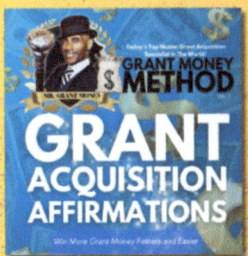
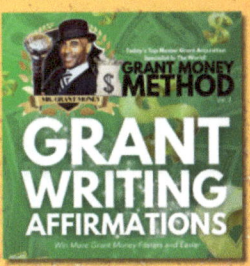

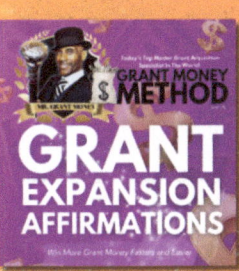

Envision and affirm your grant success in the same proactive spirit as Mr. Grant Money. **Experience the power of these daily affirmations** to inspire and motivate your journey toward success!

www.ingramcontent.com/pod-product-compliance
Lightning Source LLC
Chambersburg PA
CBHW041546220426
43665CB00002B/43